SRA Spelling Mastery

Workbook

Level D

Robert Dixon
Siegfried Engelmann

SRA
Columbus, OH

The McGraw·Hill Companies

Cover Photo Credit: Getty Images, Inc.

Illustrations: Janice Skivington

SRAonline.com

SRA

Send all inquiries to:
SRA/McGraw-Hill
4400 Easton Commons
Columbus, OH 43219-6188

ISBN 0-07-604484-X

16 17 18 19 QLM 15 14

Lesson 1

A

wander   listen   search   build   view   sort

B

1. _____ ring

2. _____ viewing

3. _____ listen

4. _____ listening

5. _____ rebuild

6. _____ searching

C

1. _____

2. _____

3. _____

4. _____

5. _____

6. _____

D

Each sentence has one misspelled word.
Write each word correctly on the blank.

1. She <u>serched</u> the <u>cloudless</u>, <u>starry</u> sky.   _____

2. Which would be the nicer <u>choise</u>, <u>swimming</u> or   _____
   <u>packing</u>?

Lesson 2

equal   cheap   straight   light   sleep   quote

B

1. _ _ _ _ t e n
2. _ _ _ _ _
3. _ u _ _ _
4. _ a _ e _
5. _ i _ w
6. _ e a _ _ _

C

1. _____
2. _____
3. _____
4. _____
5. _____
6. _____

D

Each sentence has one misspelled word.
Write each word correctly on the blank.

1. He was <u>helpfull</u> at <u>watering</u> the <u>lawn</u>.   _____

2. <u>Could</u> you make a <u>copy</u> of this <u>sine</u> for me?   _____

3. We were <u>happy</u> with the new <u>reserch</u> <u>building</u>.   _____

Lesson 3

A

spell   source   stretch   child   care   cloud

B

n   i   a   p   m   e   b   o   h   r   u   f

C

1. _ _ _ _ _ i _ h t
2. _ u _ _ e
3. _ _ _ _ t _ _ _
4. _ _ _ a l
5. _ _ g _ _
6. _ _ a _ _ _

D

1. _____
2. _____
3. _____
4. _____
5. _____
6. _____

E

Each sentence has one misspelled word.
Write each word correctly on the blank.

1. It was <u>foolish</u> to think the <u>rental</u> car would be
   <u>falltless</u>.   _____

2. We can <u>enjoy</u> this <u>deliteful</u> <u>swimming</u> pool.   _____

3. She waited <u>hopefully</u> for the <u>note</u> to arrive <u>hear</u>. _____

Lesson 4

happy	lock	study	glory	sign	people

B

1. _ _ _ _ t _ _
2. _ _ _ _ i _ h _
3. _ _ _ _ _ _
4. _ _ u _ c _
5. _ _ _ _ _
6. _ _ o _ l _

C

1. _____ + _____ = wandering
2. _____ + _____ = childless
3. _____ + _____ = misquote
4. _____ + _____ = unhappy
5. _____ + _____ = cheapest
6. _____ + _____ = resource

D

Make a small **v** above every vowel letter.
Make a small **c** above every consonant letter.

n   e   f   i   o   m   e   i   h

d   a   p   t   c   u   b   o   h

E

Cross out the misspelled words in these sentences.
Then write the words correctly above the crossed-out words.

Did you lissen to the kwote?

He did not wandor in a straite line.

Lesson 5 is a test lesson.
There is no worksheet.

Lesson 6

A

quiet   fight   break   port   school   author

B

1. _____

2. _____

3. _____

4. _____

5. _____

6. _____

C

1. quote + ing = _____

2. care + less   = _____

3. ripe + est   = _____

4. like + ness   = _____

5. stage + ing   = _____

6. fine + est   = _____

7. choke + ing = _____

8. sore + ness = _____

D

Fill in the blanks to show the morphographs in each word.

1. _____ + _____ = stretching

2. _____ + _____ = cheapest

3. _____ + _____ + _____ = rebuilding

4. _____ + _____ = darkness

5. _____ + _____ = careless

6. _____ + _____ = unhappy

E

Cross out the misspelled words in these sentences.
Then write the words correctly above the crossed-out words.

I made a careles mistake.   Some peeple sleap better than others.

Lesson 7

A

caught   picture   together   wrong

B

Please answer the question.

_____

C

1. _ u _ _ o _
2. _ _ _ e _
3. _ _ e _ _

4. _ _ o _ l _
5. _ _ h _ _ _
6. _ _ _ _ i g _ _

D

1. like + able   = _____
2. fine + est   = _____
3. ripe + ness   = _____
4. hope + less   = _____
5. stage + ing   = _____
6. cure + able   = _____

Fill in the blanks to show the morphographs in each word.

1. _____ + _____ = portable

2. _____ + _____ + _____ = remarkable

3. _____ + _____ = uneven

4. _____ + _____ = quietest

5. _____ + _____ + _____ = sleeplessness

6. _____ + _____ + _____ = unbreakable

7. _____ + _____ = searching

8. _____ + _____ = boldness

Lesson 8

A

might   story   style   voice   choice

B

1. win   3. shop   5. mad   7. star
2. sharp   4. farm   6. grab   8. port

C

__ e a s __   ___ __ w e _   ___   ___ s t ___.

_____

D

Add the morphographs together.
Some of the words follow the rule about dropping the final **e.**

1. write + ing   = _____

2. use + able   = _____

3. straight + est   = _____

4. shine + ing   = _____

5. like + ness   = _____

6. use + less   = _____

7. dark + ness   = _____

8. large + est   = _____

E

Fill in the blanks to show the morphographs in each word.

1. _____ + _____ = stretched

2. _____ + _____ + _____ = thoughtlessness

3. _____ + _____ + _____ = repainted

4. _____ + _____ = stretchable

5. _____ + _____ = mistake

6. _____ + _____ + _____ = unwashable

7. _____ + _____ + _____ = helplessness

8. _____ + _____ = clouded

F

Each sentence has one misspelled word.
Write each word correctly on the blank.

1. The <u>playful</u>, old <u>farmer</u> still has a <u>boyischness</u> to him. _____

2. The <u>golden</u> <u>sun</u> has nearly <u>rissen</u>. _____

3. As Amy was <u>skiping</u> <u>here</u>, she <u>slipped</u> and fell. _____

Lesson 9

A

thought   world   serve   grudge   charge

B

_ _ _ _ _ _ _ _ _ _ _ _ _ _ _ _ _ _ _ _ _ _ _ _ _ .

_____

C

1. slip
2. leak
3. win
4. norm
5. flat
6. drip
7. part
8. snug

D

1. _____
2. _____
3. _____
4. _____
5. _____
6. _____

E

Add the morphographs together.
Some of the words follow the rule about dropping the final **e.**

1. nice + er   = _____
2. pre + serve + ing = _____
3. ripe + ness   = _____
4. charge + ing   = _____
5. time + less   = _____
6. love + able   = _____

Lesson 10 is a test lesson.
There is no worksheet.

Lesson 11

A

busy   sailboat   noise   sketch   twice

B

1. _____

2. _____

C

Double c when cvc + v

1. run + er = _____

2. author + ing = _____

3. sad + ly = _____

4. sad + est = _____

5. swim + ing = _____

6. mad + ly = _____

7. stop + ed = _____

8. farm + er = _____

D

1. _ _ _ u _ _ _

2. _ _ y _ _

3. _ _ _ _ _ e

4. _ e _ _ _

5. _ _ _ _ _ i _ _ _

6. _ u _ _ o _

E

Add the morphographs together.
Some of the words follow the rule about
dropping the final **e.**

1. quote + able = _____

2. de + fine + ed = _____

3. use + less = _____

4. mis + shape + ed = _____

5. serve + ing = _____

6. wide + ly = _____

7. time + less = _____

8. hope + less + ly = _____

Lesson 12

A

bench   chalk   person   several   through

B

1. _____   4. _____

2. _____   5. _____

3. _____   6. _____

C

1. star + ed   = _____

2. flop + ing   = _____

3. run + ing   = _____

4. mad + ness   = _____

5. drag + ing   = _____

6. water + ing   = _____

7. big + est   = _____

8. fit + ness   = _____

D

Add the morphographs together.
Some of the words follow the rule about dropping the final **e**.

1. cure + able   = _____

2. wide + est   = _____

3. re + place + ed   = _____

4. use + able   = _____

5. un + like + ly   = _____

6. care + less   = _____

Fill in the blanks to show the morphographs in each word.

1. _____ + _____ + _____ = thoughtlessly

2. _____ + _____ = lighten

3. _____ + _____ + _____ = departed

4. _____ + _____ = straighten

5. _____ + _____ + _____ = delightful

6. _____ + _____ + _____ = unequally

Each sentence has one misspelled word.
Write each word correctly on the blank.

1. Be sure to <u>study</u> the <u>rite</u> <u>spelling</u> words.   _____

2. <u>Reveiw</u> the <u>research</u>, and then <u>write</u> the paper.   _____

3. Ann was not <u>happy</u> to see the <u>missquote</u> on her <u>sign</u>.   _____

Lesson 13

A

wreck   note   different   prove

B

1. _ _ _ _ o u _ _   4. _ _ _ _ l _

2. _ _ _ e _ a _   5. _ _ _ _ _ o _

3. _ k _ _ _ _

C

1. stop + ing   = _____

2. wrap + er   = _____

3. fit + ness   = _____

4. mad + est   = _____

5. sad + ly   = _____

6. bliss + ful = _____

7. spot + ed   = _____

8. big + est   = _____

D

1. _____ + _____ = hoping

2. _____ + _____ = finest

3. _____ + _____ = worthless

4. _____ + _____ = likable

5. _____ + _____ = useless

6. _____ + _____ = package

7. _____ + _____ = purest

8. _____ + _____ = staging

Draw a line from each word to its clue.

clothes •   • Can you _____ the music?

here •   • put words on paper

feat •   • what you wear

write •   • in this place

feet •   • correct

hear •   • His boots keep his _____ warm.

close •   • Please _____ the door when you leave.

right •   • an act of great skill

Each sentence has one misspelled word.
Write each word correctly on the blank.

1. Search for the sorce of that quote.   _____

2. The child went to sleep under a cloudles sky. _____

3. Don't worry about wrecking it as you unrap it. _____

Lesson 14

A

speak   pinch   pure

B

1. _____

_____

2. _____

_____

C

1. _____ + _____ = _____
2. _____ + _____ = _____
3. _____ + _____ = _____
4. _____ + _____ = _____
5. _____ + _____ = _____
6. _____ + _____ = _____

D

Fill in the blanks to show the morphographs in each word.

1. _____ + _____ = formal
2. _____ + _____ = package
3. _____ + _____ = thoughtful
4. _____ + _____ = quietly
5. _____ + _____ + _____ = helpfully
6. _____ + _____ = portable
7. _____ + _____ = useless
8. _____ + _____ + _____ = thoughtlessness

Add the morphographs together.
Some of the words follow the rule about dropping the final **e.**

1. fine + al = _____

2. note + able = _____

3. re + fine + ed = _____

4. un + prove + en = _____

5. serve + ing = _____

6. hope + less + ness = _____

7. charge + ing = _____

8. re + source + ful = _____

Each sentence has one misspelled word.
Write each word correctly on the blank.

1. Please keep <u>searching</u> <u>until</u> you find the <u>rippest</u> apple. _____

2. The <u>author</u> had to <u>ansser</u> six <u>questions</u>. _____

3. The <u>child</u> seems to hold a <u>gruge</u> <u>against</u> me. _____

Lesson 15 is a test lesson.
There is no worksheet.

Lesson 16

A

1. w _ _ _ _
2. _ _ _ _ e _ e _ _
3. _ e _ _ _ _
4. _ _ _ _ u _ _
5. _ _ _ a _
6. _ _ _ e _ a _

B

1. _____   4. _____
2. _____   5. _____
3. _____   6. _____

C

Add the morphographs together.
Some of the words follow the rule about doubling the final **c** in short words.

1. spin + ing   = _____
2. fool + ish   = _____
3. wrap + er   = _____
4. rent + al   = _____
5. sad + ness   = _____
6. norm + al   = _____
7. drip + ed   = _____
8. grab + ed   = _____

D

Circle the misspelled word in each group.
Then write it correctly on the line.

1. person

noize

quiet

school

_____

2. bench

light

child

sevral

_____

3. scetch

break

author

picture

_____

4. twise

chalk

prove

style

_____

5. choice

straght

might

equal

_____

6. chardge

happy

stretch

sleep

_____

E

Each sentence has one misspelled word.
Write each word correctly on the blank.

1. She has a <u>remarckable</u> <u>style</u> of <u>writing</u>.   _____

2. Was it <u>wrong</u> to <u>voice</u> what I <u>thougt</u>?   _____

3. I was <u>careless</u> with my <u>speling</u> and made a <u>mistake</u>.   _____

Lesson 17

A

1. happy   **3.** you   **5.** berry   **7.** play

2. boy   **4.** yellow   **6.** sturdy

B

1. _____   **4.** _____

2. _____   **5.** _____

3. _____   **6.** _____

C

D

1. _____ + _____ = shopper

2. _____ + _____ = running

3. _____ + _____ = fitness

4. _____ + _____ = stopped

5. _____ + _____ = planning

6. _____ + _____ = swimmer

Add the morphographs together.
The morphograph **y** is a vowel letter.

1. shine + y   = _____
2. cloud + y   = _____
3. self + ish + ly = _____
4. gum + y   = _____
5. store + age   = _____
6. rose + y   = _____
7. tribe + al   = _____
8. chop + y   = _____

Each sentence has one misspelled word.
Write each word correctly on the blank.

1. School might seem unnending by the spring.   _____
2. Please take a pitcher of us standing together.   _____
3. It helped to prevue the story.   _____

Lesson 18

A

length   strength   skate   sturdy   carry   fancy   value

B

1. _____

2. _____

3. _____

4. _____

5. _____

6. _____

C

1. _____

2. _____

3. _____

4. _____

5. _____

6. _____

D

Add the morphographs together.
The morphograph **y** is a vowel letter.

1. fur + y   = _____

2. wire + y   = _____

3. frost + y = _____

4. pup + y   = _____

5. stone + y = _____

6. dress + y = _____

Fill in the blanks to show the morphographs in each word.

1. _____ + _____ = sleepy

2. _____ + _____ = hoping

3. _____ + _____ + _____ = presented

4. _____ + _____ = saddest

5. _____ + _____ = warmest

6. _____ + _____ + _____ = selfishness

7. _____ + _____ + _____ = carelessly

8. _____ + _____ = starring

Each sentence has one misspelled word.
Write each word correctly on the blank.

1. After <u>rebiulding</u> the <u>school</u>, the workers <u>repainted</u> it.   _____

2. It was <u>remarkable</u> how brightly the <u>sun</u> was <u>shineing</u>.   _____

3. The <u>farmer</u> grew the <u>largest</u> and <u>finnest</u> pumpkins.   _____

Lesson 19

A

1. _ _ _ _ n g _ _   4. _ u _ _ _ _

2. _ _ _ _ _ _ e _ _   5. _ _ u _ _ _

3. _ _ _ _ _ _   6. _ e _ _ _

B

Fill in the blanks to show the morphographs in each word.

1. _____ + _____ + _____ = preserved

2. _____ + _____ = strengthen

3. _____ + _____ = global

4. _____ + _____ = personal

5. _____ + _____ = usage

6. _____ + _____ = biggest

7. _____ + _____ + _____ = misspelling

8. _____ + _____ = valuable

C

Cross out the misspelled words in these sentences.
Then write the words correctly above the crossed-out words.

Draw a strate line throuh each mispelling.

A buzy auther came to our skool.

D

These words are in the puzzle.
Circle 7 or more of the words.

research	answer	dark
childish	wander	light
happy	hopeless	quote
care	author	right

```
c  r  e  s  e  a  r  c  h
h  a  p  p  y  n  h  q  o
i  w  r  r  y  s  a  q  p
l  r  a  e  e  w  u  u  e
d  i  i  n  r  e  t  o  l
i  a  g  g  d  r  h  t  e
s  a  r  h  h  e  o  e  s
h  o  r  k  t  t  r  e  s
```

E

Each sentence has one misspelled word.
Write each word correctly on the blank.

1. Tom was <u>busy</u> <u>authering</u> his <u>biggest</u> book.   _____

2. It is <u>blissful</u> to sit on this <u>bench</u> on such a <u>deliteful</u> day. _____

3. Use the <u>chalk</u> to <u>darcken</u> and <u>define</u> your picture.   _____

Lesson 20 is a test lesson.
There is no worksheet.

Lesson 21

A

1. _____

2. _____

3. _____

4. _____

5. _____

6. _____

B

1. _____

2. _____

C

_____

_____

_____

_____

_____

_____

_____

_____

_____

Add the morphographs together.
Remember to use your spelling rules.

1. state + ly   = _____

2. step + ing   = _____

3. spot + less   = _____

4. safe + ly   = _____

5. style + ish   = _____

6. store + age   = _____

7. de + serve + ed = _____

8. re + fine + ed   = _____

9. win + er   = _____

10. un + plan + ed = _____

11. big + est   = _____

12. prove + ing   = _____

13. pure + ly   = _____

14. skate + ing   = _____

Each sentence has one misspelled word.
Write each word correctly on the blank.

1. The <u>rental</u> <u>saleboat</u> was a <u>wreck</u>.   _____

2. It is <u>unlikley</u> they will get <u>through</u> the <u>fitness</u> test.   _____

3. I can <u>prove</u> <u>there</u> was a note on the <u>pakkage</u>.   _____

Lesson 22

A

1. _____

2. _____

B

Add the morphographs together.

1. late + ly   = _____

2. grace + ful   = _____

3. real + ly   = _____

4. fault + less = _____

5. fire + ed   = _____

6. mis + judge   = _____

7. equal + ly   = _____

8. teach + er   = _____

C

Circle each short word that ends **cvc.**
Remember: Short words have four letters or fewer.
The letter **y** is a vowel letter at the end of a morphograph.

1. trip   5. fury   9. pass

2. joy   6. pray   10. shop

3. wander   7. drop   11. tray

4. step   8. swim   12. hit

D

Cross out the misspelled words in these sentences.
Then write the words correctly above the crossed-out words.

I like to wandor thrugh the woulds.

The speeker missquoted his sorce.

E

These words are in the puzzle.
Circle 7 or more of the words.

strength	hate	rent
stretch	rest	best
swim	mash	wash
sack	hot	catch

s	h	o	t	m	s	b	c
s	t	r	c	h	a	e	h
w	a	r	e	s	t	s	t
s	t	r	e	n	g	t	h
w	a	s	h	t	t	s	a
i	i	c	a	t	c	h	t
m	m	i	k	s	s	h	e

F

Each sentence has one misspelled word.
Write each word correctly on the blank.

1. The <u>runner</u> <u>thougtlessly</u> <u>jogged</u> through the roses. _____

2. She <u>stoppd</u> <u>twice</u> in the <u>swimming</u> race. _____

3. Mike <u>replaced</u> the <u>mishaped</u> hat with a <u>different</u> one. _____

Lesson 23

A

1. _____
2. _____
3. _____

4. _____
5. _____

B

1. _____
2. _____
3. _____
4. _____
5. _____

6. _____
7. _____
8. _____
9. _____
10. _____

C

Draw a line from each word to its clue.

vary •

whole •

hear •

hole •

here •

write •

close •

feet •

right •

clothes •

• We'll fill the _____ with dirt.

• correct

• change something

• put words on paper

• Keep your shoes on your _____.

• They left their coats _____.

• Have you read the _____ book?

• what you wear

• I don't _____ any noise.

• Please _____ the door.

D

Fill in the blanks to show the morphographs in each word.

1. _____ + _____ + _____ = carefully

2. _____ + _____ + _____ = rebuilding

3. _____ + _____ = storage

4. _____ + _____ + _____ = related

5. _____ + _____ + _____ = delightful

6. _____ + _____ = lengthy

7. _____ + _____ + _____ = restlessness

8. _____ + _____ = wrapper

9. _____ + _____ + _____ = wonderfully

10. _____ + _____ + _____ = preserved

E

Each sentence has one misspelled word.
Write each word correctly on the blank.

1. They will be <u>serving</u> <u>several</u> foods at the <u>formel</u> dinner. _____

2. They were <u>helpfull</u> at <u>fixing</u> the <u>rental</u> car. _____

3. The <u>final</u> <u>passage</u> was the <u>sadest</u> in the book. _____

Lesson 24

1. _____

2. _____

B

1. _____   4. _____

2. _____   5. _____

3. _____   6. _____

C

Make 11 real words from the morphographs in the box.

ed	er	rent	bare	ing	serve	dine

1. _____   7. _____

2. _____   8. _____

3. _____   9. _____

4. _____   10. _____

5. _____   11. _____

6. _____

D

Fill in the blanks to show the morphographs in each word.

1. _____ + _____ = shopping

2. _____ + _____ = widely

3. _____ + _____ = hopeless

4. _____ + _____ = hoping

5. _____ + _____ = runner

6. _____ + _____ = cared

Lesson 25 is a test lesson.
There is no worksheet.

Lesson 26

consonant-y + anything except i

1. study + ed = _____

2. happy + ness = _____

3. play + er = _____

4. copy + ed = _____

5. pity + ful = _____

6. deny + ed = _____

B

1. _____   **5.** _____

2. _____   **6.** _____

3. _____   **7.** _____

4. _____   **8.** _____

C

Make 15 real words from the morphographs in the box.

hope	use	ful	less	ly	care	rest

1. _____   **9.** _____

2. _____   **10.** _____

3. _____   **11.** _____

4. _____   **12.** _____

5. _____   **13.** _____

6. _____   **14.** _____

7. _____   **15.** _____

8. _____

D

Add the morphographs together.
Some of the words follow the rule about doubling the final **c** in short words.

1. big + est   = _____

2. shop + ing   = _____

3. sad + en   = _____

4. deal + er   = _____

5. run + ing   = _____

6. mad + ness   = _____

7. strength + en = _____

8. form + al + ly = _____

E

Each sentence has one misspelled word.
Write each word correctly on the blank.

1. Is it <u>normel</u> to <u>skate</u> on a <u>rainy</u> day?   _____

2. On a <u>sunny</u> day, a heavy <u>coat</u> is <u>uneeded</u>.   _____

3. I felt <u>foolish</u> in my <u>fancey</u>, <u>shiny</u> dress.   _____

Lesson 27

A

1. _____   4. _____

2. _____   5. _____

3. _____   6. _____

B

consonant-y + anything except i

1. sturdy + ness = _____

2. fury + ous   = _____

3. worry + ed   = _____

4. fancy + ful   = _____

5. play + ful   = _____

6. hurry + ed   = _____

C

_____

_____

_____

_____

_____

_____

_____

_____

Add the morphographs together.

1. style + ish = _____

2. store + age = _____

3. fine + al + ly = _____

4. re + mark + able = _____

5. un + pre + serve + ed = _____

6. mis + take + en = _____

7. de + light + ed = _____

8. gold + en = _____

9. harm + less + ly = _____

10. pre + view + ed = _____

11. quiet + est = _____

12. noise + y = _____

13. pre + date + ed = _____

14. sad + en = _____

Each sentence has one misspelled word.
Write each word correctly on the blank.

1. The <u>sleepy</u> <u>puppy</u> had <u>wirey</u> hair. _____

2. I <u>pulled</u> the <u>fury</u> dog out of the <u>hole</u>. _____

3. She <u>presented</u> the <u>swimmer</u> with a <u>shiney</u> medal. _____

Lesson 28

A

tax   box   fox

B

1. _____

2. _____

C

Write **s** or **es** in the second column.
Then add the morphographs together.

s or **es**

1. press   + _____ = _____

2. shop   + _____ = _____

3. dish   + _____ = _____

4. stretch + _____ = _____

5. goat   + _____ = _____

6. glass   + _____ = _____

D

consonant-y + anything except i

Add the morphographs together.
Some of the words follow the rule about changing **y** to **i.**

1. copy + er   = _____

2. sturdy + est   = _____

3. cry + er   = _____

4. dry + ed   = _____

5. stay + ed   = _____

6. sturdy + ness = _____

Fill in the blanks to show the morphographs in each word.

1. _____ + _____ + _____ = informal

2. _____ + _____ = disease

3. _____ + _____ = easy

4. _____ + _____ = dropping

5. _____ + _____ = package

6. _____ + _____ + _____ = formally

7. _____ + _____ = hopeless

8. _____ + _____ = hoping

Each sentence has one misspelled word.
Write each word correctly on the blank.

1. Danny carelessly dripped ink on the goldin fabric. _____

2. Finely preserved items are the most valueable. _____

3. You can strengthen your hole paper by correcting any misspelled words. _____

Lesson 29

A

1. pity + ful = _____
2. carry + ed = _____
3. fancy + est = _____
4. like + ly + est = _____
5. try + ing = _____
6. friend + ly + ness = _____
7. study + ing = _____
8. play + ful = _____

B

1. _____
2. _____
3. _____
4. _____
5. _____

6. _____
7. _____
8. _____
9. _____
10. _____

C

_____

_____

_____

_____

_____

_____

_____

_____

_____

_____

D

Write **s** or **es** in the second column.
Then add the morphographs together.

s or **es**

1. match + _____ = _____

2. tail + _____ = _____

3. pinch + _____ = _____

4. mess + _____ = _____

5. lunch + _____ = _____

6. glass + _____ = _____

7. farm + _____ = _____

8. bush + _____ = _____

E

Each sentence has one misspelled word.
Write each word correctly on the blank.

1. Our <u>teacher</u> <u>deserved</u> to be the <u>winer</u>.   _____

2. They <u>proved</u> that the <u>desiner</u> was <u>copying</u> others.   _____

3. The <u>goat</u> was <u>wunderfully</u> <u>funny</u>.   _____

Lesson 30 is a test lesson.
There is no worksheet.

Lesson 31

A

Add the morphographs together.
Follow the rule for changing **y** to **i**.

1. happy + ness = _____
2. stay + ed = _____
3. try + ed = _____
4. dry + ing = _____
5. deny + al = _____
6. hurry + ed = _____
7. vary + ed = _____
8. un + like + ly + ness = _____

B

Make 14 real words from the morphographs in the box.

de	er	fine	serve	light	ing	grade

1. _____
2. _____
3. _____
4. _____
5. _____
6. _____
7. _____
8. _____
9. _____
10. _____
11. _____
12. _____
13. _____
14. _____

C

Draw a line from each word to its clue.

whole •   • That door has a _____ in it.

vary •   • Would you come _____, please?

here •   • They wrote a _____ book.

hole •   • what you wear

clothes •   • change

very •   • The play made me feel _____ sad.

D

Add the morphographs together.

1. con + strict   = _____

2. re + in + state   = _____

3. stitch + es   = _____

4. worth + y   = _____

5. store + age   = _____

6. child + ish + ly   = _____

7. luck + y   = _____

8. con + form + ing   = _____

9. fine + al + ly   = _____

10. in + human   = _____

Lesson 32

A

leave   neat   main   claim   children

B

Whose turn is it to move?

_____

C

Add the morphographs together.
Some of the words follow the rule about changing **y** to **i.**

1. vary + ed   = _____

2. happy + est   = _____

3. spray + ed   = _____

4. friend + ly + ness = _____

5. worry + ing   = _____

6. carry + ed   = _____

D

Write **s** or **es** in the second column.
Then add the morphographs together.

                       s or **es**

1. bench   + _____ = _____

2. reach   + _____ = _____

3. box   + _____ = _____

4. wash   + _____ = _____

5. claim   + _____ = _____

6. mess   + _____ = _____

Circle the misspelled word in each group.
Then write it correctly on the line.

1. world

   cought

   shining

   wander

   _____

2. happy

   motor

   auther

   friend

   _____

3. stretch

   choice

   herb

   larje

   _____

4. equil

   change

   hopeful

   trace

   _____

5. depressing

   quiut

   human

   wrong

   _____

6. should

   would

   could

   noize

   _____

Each sentence has one misspelled word.
Write each word correctly on the blank.

1. We can't safely sail in such a pityful boat.   _____

2. The lenthy shopping trip was unplanned.   _____

3. Lately we have been dinning at really nice places.   _____

Lesson 33

A

1. _____
2. _____
3. _____
4. _____
5. _____
6. _____

7. _____
8. _____
9. _____
10. _____
11. _____
12. _____

B

W h o s e __ u r __ __ __ __ __ o __ e ?

_____

C

Fill in the blanks to show the morphographs in each word.

1. _____ + _____ = civilly

2. _____ + _____ + _____ = strengthening

3. _____ + _____ + _____ = informer

4. _____ + _____ = really

5. _____ + _____ = planning

6. _____ + _____ = changing

7. _____ + _____ + _____ = formally

8. _____ + _____ = wreckage

9. _____ + _____ + _____ = preplanned

10. _____ + _____ + _____ = hopefully

Add the morphographs together.
Some of the words follow the rule about changing **y** to **i**.

1. happy + ly   = _____

2. con + fine   = _____

3. in + side   = _____

4. girl + ish + ness   = _____

5. pity + ed   = _____

6. un + claim + ed   = _____

7. neat + ly   = _____

8. like + ly + ness   = _____

9. rain + y   = _____

10. store + age   = _____

11. norm + al + ly   = _____

12. un + drink + able = _____

13. play + ful   = _____

14. de + press + ing   = _____

15. worry + ed   = _____

Each sentence has one misspelled word.
Write each word correctly on the blank.

1. We were <u>hopeful</u> that our parade <u>flote</u> would be the <u>winner</u>. _____

2. Our <u>server</u> at the <u>dinner</u> is <u>realated</u> to me. _____

3. The <u>nice</u> girl <u>dezerved</u> a raise because she <u>cared</u> well for the plants. _____

Lesson 34

A

___ ___ <u>s e</u> ___ <u>u</u> ___ ___   ___ ___   ___ ___   ___ ___   ___ <u>o</u> ___ ___ ?

_____

B

1. _____ + _____ = _____
2. _____ + _____ = _____
3. _____ + _____ = _____
4. _____ + _____ = _____
5. _____ + _____ = _____
6. _____ + _____ = _____

C

1. _____
2. _____

D

Draw a line from each word to its clue.

lone •   • change

vary •   • put words on paper

write •   • I can _____ the music.

close •   • by yourself

hear •   • all parts together

whole •   • Don't _____ the window yet.

Write **s** or **es** in the second column.
Then add the morphographs together.

s or **es**

1. patch + _____ = _____

2. box + _____ = _____

3. claim + _____ = _____

4. class + _____ = _____

5. reach + _____ = _____

6. sign + _____ = _____

7. match + _____ = _____

8. speech + _____ = _____

Each sentence has one misspelled word.
Write each word correctly on the blank.

1. She <u>carryed</u> the <u>box</u> with both <u>arms</u>.   _____

2. John is <u>careful</u> as he <u>brushs</u> the <u>coats</u> of the animals.   _____

3. Was it <u>eazy</u> to <u>design</u> the <u>glasses</u>?   _____

> Lesson 35 is a test lesson.
> There is no worksheet.

Lesson 36

A

1. _____   4. _____

2. _____   5. _____

3. _____   6. _____

B

1. _____

2. _____

C

Figure out the rule, and write it. Remember to spell the words correctly.

and the next morphograph begins with **v** . . . when the word ends **cvc** . . .
Double the final **c** in a short word

_____

_____

D

Fill in the blanks to show the morphographs in each word.

1. _____ + _____ = cloudy

2. _____ + _____ = valuable

3. _____ + _____ = equally

4. _____ + _____ = maddest

5. _____ + _____ + _____ = reinstate

6. _____ + _____ + _____ = informer

7. _____ + _____ + _____ = preserved

8. _____ + _____ + _____ = uselessly

E

Circle the misspelled word in each group.
Then write it correctly on the line.

1. brother
   story
   shuld
   were

   _____

2. rong
   wrap
   fancy
   civil

   _____

3. shineing
   hurried
   joyful
   wander

   _____

4. stretch
   civilly
   realy
   unfilling

   _____

5. swimer
   runner
   story
   restful

   _____

6. stretcher
   friendly
   unarmmed
   shopper

   _____

F

Each sentence has one misspelled word.
Write each word correctly on the blank.

1. After dropping several items, the dealer finaly gave up. _____

2. I hurryed to finish drying the dishes. _____

3. Hopefully you'll search for hapiness. _____

Lesson 37

A

1. _ _ _ i _ _

2. _ _ _ _ _ g h _

3. _ _ i _ _ _ _ _

4. _ r _ _ _ a _ _

5. _ _ _ i _ _

6. _ _ o _ _

B

1. _____

2. _____

3. _____

4. _____

5. _____

6. _____

C

Figure out the rules, and write them. Remember to spell the words correctly.

1. a word when the next morphograph begins . . . Drop the final **e** from . . . with a vowel letter

   _____

   _____

2. **cvc** and the next . . . Double the final **c** . . . morphograph begins with **v** . . . in a short word when the word ends

   _____

   _____

D

Circle each short word that ends **cvc.**
Remember: The letter **x** acts like two consonant letters.

1. stop	4. mad	7. rent	10. box	13. boy
2. brother	5. play	8. hot	11. star	14. water
3. fox	6. buzz	9. bar	12. bare	15. snap

E

Add the morphographs together.
Some of the words follow the rule about dropping the final **e.**

1. write + ing = _____

2. in + value + able = _____

3. late + ly = _____

4. lone + ly = _____

5. force + ful + ly = _____

6. note + able = _____

7. change + ing = _____

8. re + serve + ed = _____

F

Each sentence has one misspelled word.
Write each word correctly on the blank.

1. <u>Inform</u> your <u>freinds</u> of my <u>wishes</u>.   _____

2. We <u>stayed</u> out all <u>night</u> and <u>studyed</u> the stars.   _____

3. I'm <u>tryeing</u> to put <u>plants</u> in all of the <u>rooms</u>.   _____

Lesson 38

A

1. _____

2. _____

B

1. _____ + _____ = _____

2. _____ + _____ = _____

3. _____ + _____ = _____

4. _____ + _____ = _____

5. _____ + _____ = _____

6. _____ + _____ = _____

C

1. _____   6. _____

2. _____   7. _____

3. _____   8. _____

4. _____   9. _____

5. _____   10. _____

D

Make 11 real words from the morphographs in the box.

| fine | re | sign | serve | de | con | form |

1. _____   7. _____

2. _____   8. _____

3. _____   9. _____

4. _____   10. _____

5. _____   11. _____

6. _____

E

Fill in the blanks to show the morphographs in each word.

1. _____ + _____ + _____ = remaining

2. _____ + _____ + _____ = foolishly

3. _____ + _____ = lonely

4. _____ + _____ = rainy

5. _____ + _____ + _____ + _____ = uninformed

6. _____ + _____ = conform

7. _____ + _____ + _____ = related

8. _____ + _____ = voltage

Lesson 39

A

show   grow   low   flow   throw   blow   know

B

1. _____   5. _____

2. _____   6. _____

3. _____   7. _____

4. _____   8. _____

C

1. _____ + _____ = _____

2. _____ + _____ = _____

3. _____ + _____ = _____

4. _____ + _____ = _____

5. _____ + _____ = _____

6. _____ + _____ = _____

D

_____

_____

_____

_____

_____

_____

_____

_____

Figure out the rules, and write them.

1. word ends **cvc** and . . . Double the final **c** in . . . the next morphograph
   begins with **v** . . . a short word when the

   _____

   _____

2. word when the next . . . a vowel letter . . . morphograph begins with . . .
   Drop the final **e** from a

   _____

   _____

Each sentence has one misspelled word.
Write each word correctly on the blank.

1. We <u>sprayed</u> <u>twice</u> for weeds along the <u>trial</u>.   _____

2. <u>Leave</u> the <u>paches</u> on the <u>inside</u>.   _____

3. The <u>children</u> <u>tride</u> to move the <u>boxes</u>.   _____

> Lesson 40 is a test lesson.
> There is no worksheet.

Lesson 41

A

1. _____

2. _____

B

1. _____ + _____ = _____
2. _____ + _____ = _____
3. _____ + _____ = _____
4. _____ + _____ = _____
5. _____ + _____ = _____
6. _____ + _____ = _____

C

1. Whose turn is it to make the sines? _____

2. Some people don't think that boxying is a worthy sport. _____

3. She felt sicker from crying and worring so much. _____

These words are in the puzzle.
Circle 7 or more of the words.

r	d	d	e	n	y	s
n	u	e	a	s	e	t
n	a	n	n	t	e	o
p	a	i	n	t	e	r
f	e	e	l	e	e	e
m	a	d	d	e	r	d
d	a	p	a	t	c	h

denied   patch   date

runner   ease   madder

nail   painter   stored

feel   dented   deny

Add the morphographs together.

1. un + claim + ed   = _____

2. slam + ed   = _____

3. con + fine + ing   = _____

4. in + still + ed   = _____

5. re + act +ing   = _____

6. style + ish + ly   = _____

7. con + fuse + ing   = _____

8. un + luck + y   = _____

9. fine + al   = _____

10. in + flame + ing   = _____

11. leak + age   = _____

12. un + read + able   = _____

Lesson 42

A

spray   text   tract   ruin   fluid

B

1. _ _ o w
2. _ _ r _ w
3. _ _ _ _

4. _ _ _ _
5. k _ _ _
6. _ l _ _

C

1. _____

2. _____

D

snugness   unbreakable   equally   floating

research   confuse   friendly   storage

deserve   misspelling   stepping   insure

E

1. The trapper found the trale of the foxes.   _____

2. The signs claim that the water is undrinkeable.   _____

3. I plan to confin myself to the inside today.   _____

F

Cross out the misspelled words in these sentences.
Then write the words correctly above the crossed-out words.

Pleaze cloze your books.

There is a valueable packege in the trunk.

G

Fill in the blanks to show the morphographs in each word.

1. _____ + _____ + _____ + _____ = undefeated
2. _____ + _____ + _____ = confirmed
3. _____ + _____ = moving
4. _____ + _____ + _____ = removal
5. _____ + _____ = contract
6. _____ + _____ = context
7. _____ + _____ + _____ = instated
8. _____ + _____ = sleepy
9. _____ + _____ = dosage
10. _____ + _____ + _____ = fatally

Lesson 43

A

1. _____

2. _____

B

Draw a line from each word to its clue.

loan •   • something done with great skill

weather •   • by yourself

lone •   • put words on paper

feat •   • I will _____ you my shirt.

whole •   • We can't _____ your voice.

hear •   • correct

whether •   • The _____ is good today.

write •   • change

vary •   • Do you know _____ you will go?

right •   • I ate a _____ cake.

C

Figure out the rules, and write them.

1. a word when the next . . . vowel letter . . . Drop the final **e** from . . . morphograph begins with a

   _____

   _____

2. next morphograph begins with **v** . . . the word ends **cvc** and the . . . **c** in a short word when . . . Double the final

   _____

   _____

Add the morphographs together.

1. glass + es = _____

2. race + s = _____

3. re + tract = _____

4. flat + est = _____

5. note + able = _____

6. in + cure + able = _____

7. con + fine + ing = _____

8. wreck + age = _____

9. globe + al = _____

10. con + test = _____

Each sentence has one misspelled word.
Write each word correctly on the blank.

1. She neatly put the defineing stitches on the shirt. _____

2. Figuring out your income taxses can be difficult. _____

3. The unclamed boxes varied in size. _____

A

1. _ _ _ _ y   3. _ _ _ c t   5. _ _ _ i _

2. _ _ _ _   4. _ u _ _

B

1. _____   4. _____

2. _____   5. _____

3. _____   6. _____

C

1. _____ + _____ = _____

2. _____ + _____ = _____

3. _____ + _____ = _____

4. _____ + _____ = _____

5. _____ + _____ = _____

6. _____ + _____ = _____

D

_____

_____

_____

_____

_____

_____

_____

_____

Fill in the circle marked **R** if the underlined word is spelled right.
Fill in the circle marked **W** if the underlined word is spelled wrong.

1. We have had very bad <u>weather</u> lately. Ⓡ Ⓦ

2. Are you <u>planing</u> a party? Ⓡ Ⓦ

3. That was a <u>realy</u> funny story. Ⓡ Ⓦ

4. I <u>thought</u> we won the race. Ⓡ Ⓦ

5. My sister <u>wrote</u> me a long note. Ⓡ Ⓦ

6. Have you <u>studyed</u> for the test? Ⓡ Ⓦ

Each sentence has one misspelled word.
Write each word correctly on the blank.

1. I get depresed easily in bad weather. _____

2. It's pointless for her to growe long nails. _____

3. Don't blow on it; it's quite brakeable. _____

> Lesson 45 is a test lesson.
> There is no worksheet.

Lesson 46

A

Our yellow flowers bloomed early.

_____

B

1. _____ + _____ = _____
2. _____ + _____ = _____
3. _____ + _____ = _____
4. _____ + _____ = _____
5. _____ + _____ = _____
6. _____ + _____ = _____

C

Add the morphographs together.

1. con + text = _____
2. ruin + ed = _____
3. con + tract = _____
4. lone + ly = _____
5. un + de + feat + ed = _____
6. fine + al + ly = _____
7. person + al + ly = _____
8. watch + es = _____
9. noise + y = _____
10. trail + er = _____

These words are in the puzzle.
Circle 7 or more of the words.

throw	error	threw
house	large	worry
reach	storage	teach
caught	cure	eight

s	c	a	u	g	h	t
t	t	w	c	c	t	e
e	h	o	u	s	e	a
i	r	r	r	r	r	c
g	o	r	e	a	c	h
h	w	y	o	w	g	a
t	t	l	a	r	g	e

Each sentence has one misspelled word.
Write each word correctly on the blank.

1. A few reserved seats were remaning for the show. _____

2. I know it's incureable, but I'm unclear as to why. _____

3. The sturdiest rail was foolishley taken down. _____

Lesson 47

A

cause   pause   poison   strange

B

1. _____

2. _____

3. _____

4. _____

5. _____

6. _____

C

Ou_ ye_l_w __ow___ __oo_e_ ear___.

_____

D

1. _____

2. _____

3. _____

4. _____

5. _____

6. _____

E

Add the morphographs together.
Some of the words follow the rule about changing **y** to **i.**

1. worry + ed   = _____

2. pity + ful   = _____

3. study + ing   = _____

4. play + ful + ly   = _____

5. boy + ish + ness = _____

6. try + ed   = _____

7. fancy + ful   = _____

Lesson 48

A

1. _____

2. _____

B

1. _ _ u _ _ _

2. _ a _ s _

3. _ _ _ u g _ _

4. _ o _ _ o _

5. _ a _ _ _

6. _ _ r _ n g _

C

_ u _ y _ _ _ w _ _ o w _ _ _ _ _ _ o _ _ _

e a _ _ _ _ .

_____

D

_____

_____

_____

_____

_____

_____

_____

Fill in the blanks to show the morphographs in each word.

1. _____ + _____ = strangely

2. _____ + _____ = consent

3. _____ + _____ + _____ = presented

4. _____ + _____ + _____ = misplaced

5. _____ + _____ + _____ = winners

6. _____ + _____ + _____ = invaluable

7. _____ + _____ = wonderful

8. _____ + _____ + _____ = reserved

Each sentence has one misspelled word.
Write each word correctly on the blank.

1. Conserve your money, and let it grow, or you'll
   need a lone.   _____

2. Put down that container you're carying.   _____

3. The whether forcefully reshaped the land.   _____

Lesson 49

___ __y_____ __w___ _____ _a____.

_____

B

1. _____   4. _____

2. _____   5. _____

3. _____   6. _____

C

Draw a line from each word to its clue.

weather •   • by yourself

loan •   • ordinary

plain •   • Let's decide _____ or not we will go.

right •   • Today's _____ is fine.

lone •   • change

whether •   • Please _____ me some paint.

vary •   • I have a _____ in my shoe.

hole •   • You gave the _____ answer.

D

Add the morphographs together.
Remember to use your spelling rules.

1. early + est = _____

2. con + fine + ment = _____

3. happy + est = _____

4. cloud + y + ness = _____

5. scratch + es = _____

6. pay + ment = _____

7. dark + ness = _____

8. strange + est = _____

9. tough + est = _____

10. grace + ful + ly = _____

E

Each sentence has one misspelled word.
Write each word correctly on the blank.

1. Todd hopped he would win the baking contest. _____

2. The text is so confusing that it's unreadabal. _____

3. The leeder in all the races is still undefeated. _____

Lesson 50 is a test lesson.
There is no worksheet.

Lesson 51

A

1. brain	**3.** drain	**5.** plain	**7.** sprain
2. chain	**4.** gain	**6.** rain	**8.** stain

B

1. _____

2. _____

C

1. _____   **4.** _____

2. _____   **5.** _____

3. _____   **6.** _____

D

Fill in the blanks to show the morphographs in each word.

1. _____ + _____ = stained

2. _____ + _____ = basement

3. _____ + _____ = strangeness

4. _____ + _____ = questionable

5. _____ + _____ = flattest

6. _____ + _____ + _____ = inflaming

E

Circle the misspelled word in each group.
Then write it correctly on the line.

1. cloudy
   contract
   pichure
   question

   _____

2. stranger
   driping
   whose
   leader

   _____

3. flowers
   yello
   pause
   regain

   _____

4. lenghten
   package
   movement
   caught

   _____

5. relate
   wonderful
   poisen
   speaker

   _____

6. through
   eight
   people
   helplesness

   _____

7. misspelled
   ruined
   equaly
   mistake

   _____

8. cawze
   valuable
   resources
   confused

   _____

F

Each sentence has one misspelled word.
Write each word correctly on the blank.

1. Lateley I have been reading some notable letters.   _____

2. She forcefully denied that she was moveing.   _____

3. The researcher was confuseed by both parts of the study.   _____

Lesson 52

_____

_____

_____

_____

_____

_____

_____

_____

spotted	boxes	pause	rainy	straightest
quotable	happiness	yellow	contract	wonderful
throat	cheapest	trail	cause	ruined
together	graceful	speeches	early	resourceful
pleasing	studying	blowing	strange	speaker

Fill in the blanks to show the morphographs in each word.

1. _____ + _____ + _____ = department

2. _____ + _____ + _____ = confinement

3. _____ + _____ + _____ + _____ = unconfirmed

4. _____ + _____ + _____ = investment

5. _____ + _____ = lucky

6. _____ + _____ = voltage

7. _____ + _____ + _____ = normally

8. _____ + _____ = valuable

9. _____ + _____ + _____ = delightful

Each sentence has one misspelled word.
Write each word correctly on the blank.

1. Instead of sleeping, he studeyed his music lesson.   _____

2. By waterring their lawn, they are changing the water   _____
   force.

3. The picture is covered by unbrekable glass.   _____

Lesson 53

1. _____

2. _____

B

Figure out the rules, and write them.

1. in a word when the . . . next morphograph begins with . . . word ends consonant-and-**y** and the . . . Change the **y** to **i** . . . anything except **i**

   _____

   _____

2. with a **v** . . . morphograph begins . . . word when the next . . . Drop the final **e** from a

   _____

   _____

C

Add the morphographs together.
Remember to use your spelling rules.

1. luck + y + ly   = _____

2. early + er   = _____

3. strange + er   = _____

4. fine + al + ly   = _____

5. friend + ly + ness   = _____

6. flat + en   = _____

7. re + late + ed   = _____

8. in + vest + ment + s   = _____

9. source + es   = _____

10. cloud + y + est   = _____

Lesson 54

A

1. _____
2. _____
3. _____

4. _____
5. _____
6. _____

B

_____
_____
_____
_____
_____
_____
_____
_____
_____

C

Make 10 real words from the morphographs in the box.

en	est	sad	mad	ness	wide	fine

1. _____
2. _____
3. _____
4. _____
5. _____

6. _____
7. _____
8. _____
9. _____
10. _____

Fill in the blanks to show the morphographs in each word.

1. _____ + _____ = stranger

2. _____ + _____ = taken

3. _____ + _____ = choicest

4. _____ + _____ = forceful

5. _____ + _____ = signal

6. _____ + _____ + _____ = resigned

7. _____ + _____ + _____ = contracted

8. _____ + _____ + _____ = consignment

9. _____ + _____ + _____ + _____ = unmistakable

10. _____ + _____ + _____ = wonderfully

Each sentence has one misspelled word.
Write each word correctly on the blank.

1. The new design made some people feel lonly. _____

2. He denyed removing the contract from our safe. _____

3. He became sleepy as he floted on the raft. _____

Lesson 55 is a test lesson.
There is no worksheet.

Lesson 56

A

1. _____

2. _____

B

Make 14 real words from the morphographs in the box.

fine	con	de	re	ment	move	ing	ed

1. _____   8. _____

2. _____   9. _____

3. _____   10. _____

4. _____   11. _____

5. _____   12. _____

6. _____   13. _____

7. _____   14. _____

C

These words are in the puzzle.
Circle 7 or more of the words.

civil   verb   carry

might   deny   robber

gone   dine   match

mad   does   easy

c	i	v	i	l	r
m	a	d	e	r	o
a	i	r	i	r	b
t	d	g	r	n	b
c	e	o	h	y	e
h	n	n	e	t	r
m	y	e	a	s	y

D

Add the morphographs together.
Some of the words follow the rule about changing **y** to **i**.

1. boy + ish   = _____
2. sturdy + ness   = _____
3. worry + ed   = _____
4. pity + ful   = _____
5. sign + al   = _____
6. carry + er   = _____
7. cry + ing   = _____
8. try + al   = _____
9. deny + al   = _____
10. fly + er   = _____

Lesson 57

A

Write contractions for the words below.

1. could not = _____

2. should not = _____

3. she is   = _____

4. is not   = _____

5. he will   = _____

6. would not = _____

7. I have   = _____

8. you will   = _____

B

1. _____

2. _____

3. _____

4. _____

5. _____

6. _____

C

Carrying the heavy load is sure to make me breathe hard.

_____

_____

D

Circle the misspelled word in each group.
Then write it correctly on the line.

1. other
   wonderfull
   wrong
   could
   _____

2. story
   mispell
   sturdy
   fancy
   _____

3. yellow
   strength
   serve
   strech
   _____

4. author
   poison
   saddness
   civil
   _____

5. dripping
   enuff
   pitch
   normal
   _____

6. peeple
   delightful
   rebuild
   while
   _____

7. valeu
   unthinking
   date
   coldest
   _____

8. useless
   wanted
   worrying
   frends
   _____

Lesson 58

A

Write contractions for the words below.

1. were not   = _____   **5.** you have   = _____

2. does not   = _____   **6.** did not   = _____

3. are not   = _____   **7.** can not   = _____

4. she will   = _____   **8.** they are   = _____

B

_ a _ r y _ _ _ _   _ _ _   _ e a _ y   _ o a _   _ _

s u r _   _ _   _ _ k _   _ _   _ _ e a _ _ e   _ a _ _ .

_____

_____

C

Make 10 real words from the morphographs in the box.

pity	er	ed	fancy	ful	ing	play

1. _____   **6.** _____

2. _____   **7.** _____

3. _____   **8.** _____

4. _____   **9.** _____

5. _____   **10.** _____

D

Add the morphographs together.

1. catch + es = _____

2. mis + print + ed = _____

3. un + snap + ed = _____

4. point + less = _____

5. re + serve + ed = _____

6. fit + ness = _____

7. de + light + ful = _____

8. un + de + feat + ed = _____

9. un + vary + ed = _____

10. leak + age = _____

11. speed + y + est = _____

12. ship + ment = _____

13. in + tend + ed = _____

14. con + front = _____

E

Each sentence has one misspelled word.
Write each word correctly on the blank.

1. Five mice will be raceing in the contest. _____

2. She tryed to find her way out of the darkness. _____

3. When did you consent to this wonderfull plan? _____

Lesson 59

A

1. _____

2. _____

B

_ a _ _ y _ _ _ _ _ _ _ _ e a _ _ _ _ _ _ _ _ _

_ u r _ _ _ _ _ _ _ _ _ _ _ _ _ e a _ _ e _ _ _ _ .

_____

_____

C

Write the word for each meaning.
The words will contain these morphographs.

al—related to   **ful**—full of   **est**—the most

pre—before   **ish**—like   **en**—make

1. _____ like a baby

2. _____ the most late

3. _____ related to signs

4. _____ wrap before

5. _____ make light

6. _____ full of care

D

Write contractions for the words below.

1. let us   = _____

2. have not = _____

3. was not   = _____

4. they will = _____

5. we have   = _____

6. what is   = _____

7. he is   = _____

8. would not = _____

E

Add the morphographs together.

1. swim + er   = _____

2. fine + est   = _____

3. wide + est   = _____

4. con + sign   = _____

5. mad + ly   = _____

6. rage + ing   = _____

7. trap + er   = _____

8. un + civil + ly   = _____

Lesson 60 is a test lesson.
There is no worksheet.

Lesson 61

A

_ _ _ _ _ _ _ _ _   _ _ _   _ _ a _ _   _ _ _ _   _ _

_ _ _ _   _ _ _ _   _ _ _ _   _ _   _ _ _ _ _ _   e _ _ _ _.

_____

_____

B

Complete each sentence correctly with one of these words:

write   **right**

1. My grandmother likes it when I _____ long letters.

2. Janis is the _____ person for the job.

3. My answers on the test were all _____.

4. When Martin was four years old, he could _____ his name.

C

Write contractions for the words below.

1. has not   = _____   5. I will   = _____

2. you are   = _____   6. they are   = _____

3. we will   = _____   7. were not   = _____

4. are not   = _____   8. it is   = _____

Circle the misspelled word in each group.
Then write it correctly on the line.

1. worry	2. catch	3. hurring	4. claim
might	friend	fitness	queit
brother	wandor	preview	choice
civel	change	ruined	equal

_____ _____ _____ _____

Fill in the blanks to show the morphographs in each word.

1. _____ + _____ + _____ + _____ = unrefined

2. _____ + _____ + _____ = packaging

3. _____ + _____ + _____ = rightfully

4. _____ + _____ = inhuman

5. _____ + _____ + _____ = strengthening

6. _____ + _____ + _____ = loneliness

7. _____ + _____ + _____ = helplessness

8. _____ + _____ + _____ = unequally

9. _____ + _____ + _____ = resigned

10. _____ + _____ + _____ + _____ = unrelated

Lesson 62

A

1. _____

_____

2. _____

B

1. _____   5. _____

2. _____   6. _____

3. _____   7. _____

4. _____   8. _____

C

Write contractions for the words below.

1. should not = _____   4. what is   = _____

2. she is   = _____   5. they will = _____

3. I have   = _____   6. we are   = _____

D

Complete each sentence correctly with one of these words:

weather   clothes   very   sale   would

1. Are those toys for _____?

2. That rack is _____ heavy.

3. The _____ has been cold and rainy all week.

4. Do you know which _____ he wore?

5. I _____ stay longer if I had more time.

6. Our spelling test was _____ easy.

Figure out the rules, and write them.

1. in a short word when the . . . next morphograph begins with **v** . . . Double the final **c** . . . word ends **cvc** and the

_____

_____

2. consonant-and-**y** and the . . . a word when the word ends . . . next morphograph begins with anything except **i** . . . Change the **y** to **i** in

_____

_____

Each sentence has one misspelled word.
Write each word correctly on the blank.

1. The fish seemed confused and was spining around in the water. _____

2. Such a large dosege is unproven and may be harmful. _____

3. They were hopeful as they planed a delightful party. _____

Lesson 63

A

1. _____ + _____ = _____
2. _____ + _____ = _____
3. _____ + _____ = _____
4. _____ + _____ = _____
5. _____ + _____ = _____
6. _____ + _____ = _____
7. _____ + _____ = _____
8. _____ + _____ = _____

B

1. _____

_____

2. _____

_____

C

Make 11 real words from the morphographs in the box.

friend	ly	happy	ness	lone	sturdy	est

1. _____
2. _____
3. _____
4. _____
5. _____
6. _____

7. _____
8. _____
9. _____
10. _____
11. _____

D

Write contractions for the words below.

1. can not = _____
2. does not = _____
3. they will = _____
4. you have = _____

5. are not = _____
6. what is = _____
7. it is = _____
8. let us = _____

E

Fill in the blanks to show the morphographs in each word.

1. _____ + _____ = sadder
2. _____ + _____ = strengthen
3. _____ + _____ + _____ = informal
4. _____ + _____ = useful
5. _____ + _____ = express
6. _____ + _____ + _____ = reserving
7. _____ + _____ + _____ = defacing
8. _____ + _____ = planning

There are no worksheets for
Lesson 64 and Lesson 65.

Lesson 66

1. _____ + _____ = _____
2. _____ + _____ = _____
3. _____ + _____ = _____
4. _____ + _____ = _____
5. _____ + _____ = _____
6. _____ + _____ = _____
7. _____ + _____ = _____
8. _____ + _____ = _____

B

Add the morphographs together.

1. re + move + al = _____

2. in + come = _____

3. rise + ing = _____

4. safe + ly = _____

5. hot + est = _____

6. mad + ness = _____

7. un + de + serve + ing = _____

8. use + age = _____

9. verb + al + ly = _____

10. re + cent + ly = _____

11. swim + er = _____

12. real + ly = _____

D

Cross out the misspelled words in these sentences.
Then write the words correctly above the crossed-out words.

Sevral stranje birds landed togather.

We are'nt leaving the main road.

That was the greatest feet of strenght I've seen.

Lesson 67

A

1. _____
2. _____
3. _____
4. _____
5. _____
6. _____

B

1. _ _ O _ _ _
2. _ _ _ U _
3. _ _ U _ _ _
4. _ _ _ _ _
5. _ _ _ W _
6. _ _ _ _ _

C

These words are in the puzzle.
Circle 7 or more of the words.

brotherly   stay   report

spotted   vary   race

neat   length   traps

loud   whether   cared

b	r	c	l	s	n	t	l	w
r	r	n	a	o	u	u	e	h
s	e	o	n	r	u	o	n	e
s	p	o	t	t	e	d	g	t
s	o	a	y	h	n	d	t	h
s	r	a	c	e	e	e	h	e
l	t	r	a	p	s	r	a	r
v	t	a	t	o	r	t	l	t
v	a	r	y	y	r	h	h	y

D

Complete each sentence correctly with these words:

weather   **vary**   **write**   **they're**   **right**   **whole**

1. Tony's new shoes are exactly the _____ size.

2. Instead of eating the same thing all the time, you should _____ your diet.

3. My uncle was so hungry last Sunday that he ate a _____ chicken.

4. The farmers aren't worried. _____ expecting good _____.

5. Joggers don't usually run at the same speed all the time. They usually _____ their pace.

6. The blanks on your worksheet are where you _____ spelling words.

7. Last Friday we worked the _____ day.

E

Each sentence has one misspelled word.
Write each word correctly on the blank.

1. Our investments were confirmed to be very valueble. _____

2. Who wrote the best ansuers to the questions? _____

3. What caused you to buy that strange painte? _____

Lesson 68

A

quick   quiz   quest

B

1. _____

2. _____

C

1. _____ 5. _____

2. _____ 6. _____

3. _____ 7. _____

4. _____ 8. _____

D

Write **s** or **es** in the second column.
Then add the morphographs together.

s or **es**

1. glass   + _____ = _____

2. reach   + _____ = _____

3. sound   + _____ = _____

4. brush   + _____ = _____

5. scratch + _____ = _____

6. flower + _____ = _____

Fill in the blanks to show the morphographs in each word.

1. _____ + _____ + _____ = explained

2. _____ + _____ = resource

3. _____ + _____ = movement

4. _____ + _____ + _____ + _____ = unrelated

5. _____ + _____ + _____ + _____ = unconfirmed

6. _____ + _____ + _____ = informer

7. _____ + _____ + _____ = childishly

8. _____ + _____ + _____ = noisiness

Each sentence has one misspelled word.
Write each word correctly on the blank.

1. The flowers and birds made a lovely pickture together. _____

2. The movment of the ship caused me to feel dizzy. _____

3. After twenty years she finaly said that she would resign. _____

Lesson 69

A

1. _ _ _ e _

2. _ u _ _

3. _ _ e _ _

4. _ _ _ t _

5. _ _ o _ _

6. _ _ _ c _

B

_____

_____

_____

_____

_____

_____

_____

_____

_____

C

their •

here •

vary •

close •

sale •

loan •

they're •

write •

feet •

weather •

• She forgot to _____ the window.

• contraction of **they are**

• Can you _____ me some money?

• The students exchanged _____ papers.

• change

• The _____ has been good lately.

• My _____ were sore after the hike.

• We moved _____ a year ago.

• Our car is for _____.

• I can _____ two words in Spanish.

Cross out the misspelled words in these sentences.
Then write the words correctly above the crossed-out words.

We worryed uselesly about the whether.

My frend chandges his cloze offen.

Lesson 70 is a test lesson.
There is no worksheet.

Lesson 71

A

One athlete finished the contest before everyone else.

_____

_____

B

1. _____

2. _____

3. _____

4. _____

5. _____

6. _____

7. _____

8. _____

9. _____

10. _____

11. _____

12. _____

C

Write contractions for the words below.

1. it is   = _____

2. are not   = _____

3. that is   = _____

4. would not   = _____

5. can not   = _____

6. let us   = _____

7. you will   = _____

8. we have   = _____

D

Add the morphographs together.

1. re + quest = _____

2. win + er = _____

3. pity + ful = _____

4. strength + en + ing = _____

5. un + ex + plain + ed = _____

6. de + feat + ed = _____

7. re + place + ment = _____

8. con + front + ed = _____

9. nudge + ing = _____

10. star + ing = _____

11. ripe + ness = _____

12. straight + est = _____

E

Each sentence has one misspelled word.
Write each word correctly on the blank.

1. It is unlikely that they will remain peacful. _____

2. They presented questions about the leakags from the pipes. _____

3. Which department store serves the best refereshments? _____

Lesson 72

A

O_e ___lete ___ish_d ___ __n__st __f__re __ve_yo__ e_se.

_____

_____

B

_____

_____

_____

_____

_____

_____

_____

_____

C

Make 9 real words from the morphographs in the box.

ed	form	re	in	er	con

1. _____

2. _____

3. _____

4. _____

5. _____

6. _____

7. _____

8. _____

9. _____

Figure out the rules, and write them.

1. in a short word when the . . . Double the final **c** . . . morphograph begins with **v** . . . word ends **cvc** and the next

_____

_____

2. with anything except **i** . . . and the next morphograph begins . . . when the word ends consonant-and-**y** . . . to **i** in a word . . . Change the **y**

_____

_____

Lesson 73

A

danger   beauty   sudden   cover

B

1. _____

2. _____

C

1. _____   5. _____

2. _____   6. _____

3. _____   7. _____

4. _____   8. _____

D

Write the contractions for the words below.

1. could not = _____

2. it is   = _____

3. are not   = _____

4. we will   = _____

5. you will   = _____

6. let us   = _____

7. you have   = _____

8. does not   = _____

Draw a line from each word to its clue.

peace •   • by yourself

their •   • belonging to them

whole •   • We think _____ coming home soon.

lone •   • no fighting

they're •   • My answer wasn't _____.

right •   • We ate a _____ loaf of bread.

Each sentence has one misspelled word.
Write each word correctly on the blank.

1. We thought that they caught seaveral fish.   _____

2. She is a resourcful shopper and makes wise   _____
   investments.

3. The early reports about the risks of ruining the land _____
   were misstaken.

Lesson 74

A

1. _ e a _ _ _

2. _ u _ _ _ _

3. _ _ _ e _

4. _ _ _ g _ _

5. _ _ _ d _ _

6. q _ _ _ _

B

1. _____

2. _____

3. _____

4. _____

5. _____

6. _____

7. _____

8. _____

9. _____

10. _____

C

Cross out the misspelled words in these sentences.
Then write the words correctly above the crossed-out words.

There arn't enugh resorces for that plan.

The happyest childern wern't realy rich.

Write **s** or **es** in the second column.
Then add the morphographs together.

s or **es**

1. world   + _____ = _____

2. stretch   + _____ = _____

3. research + _____ = _____

4. wash   + _____ = _____

5. light   + _____ = _____

6. tax   + _____ = _____

7. class   + _____ = _____

8. refresh   + _____ = _____

E

Complete each sentence correctly with one of these words:

write   **right**

1. Do you have the _____ time?

2. I started to _____ my report early.

3. Be sure to _____ your name on all your work.

4. We finally found the _____ house.

5. My dad has a scar on his _____ hand.

Lesson 75 is a test lesson.
There is no worksheet.

Lesson 76

A

O__ ____ete ____is___ ___
_____s ___ore __ery _e ___e.

_____

_____

B

1. _____   5. _____

2. _____   6. _____

3. _____   7. _____

4. _____   8. _____

C

_____

_____

_____

_____

_____

_____

_____

D

Fill in the blanks to show the morphographs in each word.

1. _____ + _____ + _____ = confinement
2. _____ + _____ + _____ = wonderfully
3. _____ + _____ + _____ = requesting
4. _____ + _____ + _____ = unquotable
5. _____ + _____ + _____ = explained
6. _____ + _____ = stranger
7. _____ + _____ = poisoning
8. _____ + _____ = context
9. _____ + _____ + _____ = cloudiness

E

Each sentence has one misspelled word.
Write each word correctly on the blank.

1. We were impressed with the friendlyness of the _____
   stranger.

2. Some people like to go shoping on the cloudiest days. _____

3. You can clearly hear her greatness in her speechs. _____

Lesson 77

chief   niece   grief   brief   thief

B

_ _ _ _ _ _ _ _ e t e _ _ _ _ _ _ e _ _ _ _

_ _ _ _ _ _ _ _ _ o r e _ _ e _ y _ _ _ _ _ _ _ .

_____

_____

C

D

Add the morphographs together.
Remember to use your spelling rules.

1. beauty + ful = _____

2. sudden + ly = _____

3. peace + ful + ly = _____

4. ex + change + ing = _____

5. in + vest + ment = _____

6. con + tact + ed = _____

7. re + strict + ed = _____

8. noise + y = _____

9. fine + al + ly = _____

10. volt + age = _____

11. grip + ing = _____

Lesson 78

A

_ _ _   _ _ _ _ _ _   e _ e   _ _ _ _ _ _ _ _   _ _ _

_ _ _ _ _ _ _   _ _ _   e   _ _ e _ _ _ _   _ _ _ _ .

_____

_____

B

1. _ r _ e _

2. _ i _ c _

3. _ _ i _ _

4. _ _ _ _ _ _

5. _ h _ _ _

C

_____

_____

_____

_____

_____

_____

_____

_____

Circle the misspelled word in each group.
Then write it correctly on the line.

1. worryed

    crying

    denied

    playful

    _____

2. chalky

    children

    cheepest

    changing

    _____

3. spotless

    maddness

    winner

    shopping

    _____

4. straight

    stretch

    strenght

    switch

    _____

5. really

    filling

    nicely

    civily

    _____

6. thought

    enough

    thrugh

    question

    _____

Each sentence has one misspelled word.
Write each word correctly on the blank.

1. His plan might riune the delightful trail.   _____

2. They were not joyful as they studyed the report.   _____

3. She greatly improved the wraping paper.   _____

Lesson 79

A

govern   reason   type   house   first

B

1. _____
2. _____
3. _____
4. _____

5. _____
6. _____
7. _____
8. _____

C

1. _____

_____

2. _____

D

Fill in the blanks to show the morphographs in each word.

1. _____ + _____ + _____ = defining
2. _____ + _____ = final
3. _____ + _____ + _____ = confinement
4. _____ + _____ + _____ = designer
5. _____ + _____ + _____ = resigned
6. _____ + _____ = signal
7. _____ + _____ + _____ + _____ = unrecoverable
8. _____ + _____ = heaviest

E

Circle the short **cvc** words.

Remember: Short words have four letters or fewer.

The letter **y** is a vowel letter at the end of a morphograph.

The letter **x** acts like two consonant letters.

1. sudden   4. trip   7. grab   10. reason

2. boy   5. poison   8. spot   11. cover

3. chin   6. box   9. hid   12. flat

Lesson 80 is a test lesson.
There is no worksheet.

A

1. _ y _ _ _

2. _ i _ _ _

3. _ o _ e r _

4. _ e a _ o _

5. _ _ u s _

B

1. _____

_____

2. _____

_____

C

1. _____

2. _____

3. _____

4. _____

5. _____

6. _____

D

Complete each sentence correctly with one of these words.

peace   **there**   **they're**   **piece**   **their**

1. The boys are staying home because _____ sick.

2. Please put those books over _____ , on the shelf.

3. Someone gave us each a _____ of pie.

4. I enjoy the _____ and quiet of the lake.

5. Mr. and Mrs. Sato lost _____ dog.

6. We all wrote a thank-you note on one _____ of paper.

7. Matt and Kim went fishing yesterday. _____ going again today.

8. I went to your house, but you weren't _____ .

Lesson 82

A

Our second surprise was especially exciting.

_____

_____

B

s or **es**   **s** or **es**

1. worry + _____ = _____   6. boy   + _____ = _____

2. story + _____ = _____   7. play   + _____ = _____

3. try   + _____ = _____   8. study + _____ = _____

4. joy   + _____ = _____   9. stay   + _____ = _____

5. copy   + _____ = _____   10. carry + _____ = _____

C

Circle the misspelled word in each group.
Then write it correctly on the line.

1. proud	2. wander	3. auther
strength	equil	hurry
mispelled	answer	sturdy
wrong	friendly	reason
_____	_____	_____

4. pleaze	5. danger	6. rezerve
straight	should	house
whose	happiness	swimmer
niece	realy	chief
_____	_____	_____

Lesson 83

A

___ ___co_d __ur__ise ___
e__ecial_ _xc_t_ng.

_____

_____

B

s or **es**   **s** or **es**

1. stay + _____ = _____   **5.** worry + _____ = _____

2. copy + _____ = _____   **6.** fly   + _____ = _____

3. toy   + _____ = _____   **7.** boy   + _____ = _____

4. spray + _____ = _____   **8.** carry + _____ = _____

C

Fill in the blanks to show the morphographs in each word.

1. _____ + _____ + _____ = prolonged

2. _____ + _____ = express

3. _____ + _____ + _____ = profoundly

4. _____ + _____ + _____ = refinement

5. _____ + _____ + _____ = exported

6. _____ + _____ = conserve

7. _____ + _____ + _____ + _____ = unrelated

8. _____ + _____ = briefly

Add the morphographs together.

1. govern + ment = _____
2. rise + ing = _____
3. trap + ed = _____
4. straight + en = _____
5. reason + able = _____
6. un + type + ed = _____
7. carry + ed = _____
8. strength + en = _____
9. force + ful = _____
10. beauty + ful + ly = _____

Each sentence has one misspelled word.
Write each word correctly on the blank.

1. How many people are in the buisness of exporting food? _____
2. She presented us with a wunderful display of flowers. _____
3. How did the boxes of brushs get in the bushes? _____

A

_ __ ___o__ __r___s_ ___
____cia___ _xc_____.

_____

_____

B

s or **es**

1. boy   + ____ = _____
2. story   + ____ = _____
3. try   + ____ = _____
4. worry   + ____ = _____
5. stay   + ____ = _____
6. fly   + ____ = _____
7. study   + ____ = _____
8. carry   + ____ = _____

C

shouldn't	caught	replacement	chiefly	watching
together	believe	answer	house	conserve
different	exchange	govern	greatest	school
children	safely	person	signal	hurried

Complete each sentence correctly with these words:

would   **write**   **they're**   **whole**   **their**

very   **vary**   **right**   **hole**

1. Parachute jumping is a _____ exciting sport.

2. Whenever you misspell a word, you should _____ that word correctly at least one time.

3. A woodpecker made a small _____ in the side of our barn.

4. The boys are late because _____ helping Mrs. Olmsted.

5. No one thought Sandy _____ finish her book, but she read the _____ story anyway.

6. The Marche Company hasn't hired a shipping clerk because they haven't found the _____ person for the job.

7. I do different exercises every day. My friends also _____ _____ exercises.

Lesson 85 is a test lesson.
There is no worksheet.

Lesson 86

s or **es**

1. study + _____ = _____
2. story + _____ = _____
3. play + _____ = _____
4. glory + _____ = _____
5. cry + _____ = _____
6. joy + _____ = _____
7. city + _____ = _____
8. fly + _____ = _____

B

1. _____
   _____
2. _____

C

1. _____   4. _____
2. _____   5. _____
3. _____   6. _____

listen   proclaim   reason   style

largest   sleepy   search   picture

school   pitiful   question   straight

Make 11 real words from the morphographs in the box.

| hot | ly | sturdy | er | mad | nasty | est |

1. _____   7. _____

2. _____   8. _____

3. _____   9. _____

4. _____   10. _____

5. _____   11. _____

6. _____

Each sentence has one misspelled word.
Write each word correctly on the blank.

1. Our restlessness grew because of the countles delays. _____

2. The noise they made proved how thougtless they are. _____

3. The speeker misquoted the remarks we made. _____

There is no worksheet for
Lesson 87.

Lesson 88

A

1. show   **2.** water   **3.** know   **4.** law   **5.** whether   **6.** blow

B

s or **es**   **s** or **es**

1. copy + _____ = _____   **5.** city + _____ = _____

2. spray + _____ = _____   **6.** worry + _____ = _____

3. fly + _____ = _____   **7.** study + _____ = _____

4. boy + _____ = _____   **8.** story + _____ = _____

C

Write contractions for the words below.

1. were not = _____   **5.** let us = _____

2. have not = _____   **6.** are not = _____

3. you will = _____   **7.** would not = _____

4. they had = _____   **8.** does not = _____

D

Fill in the blanks to show the morphographs in each word.

1. _____ + _____ = relate

2. _____ + _____ + _____ = relative

3. _____ + _____ + _____ = expressive

4. _____ + _____ = moving

5. _____ + _____ + _____ = removal

6. _____ + _____ = proverb

7. _____ + _____ = react

8. _____ + _____ + _____ = reaction

Lesson 89

A

1. _____

2. _____

B

1. _____ 4. _____

2. _____ 5. _____

3. _____ 6. _____

C

_____

_____

_____

_____

_____

_____

_____

_____

_____

D

Write **s** or **es** in the second column. Then add the morphographs together.

s or **es**

1. tax + _____ = _____
2. study + _____ = _____
3. play + _____ = _____
4. brush + _____ = _____
5. reason + _____ = _____
6. copy + _____ = _____
7. thought + _____ = _____
8. worry + _____ = _____
9. spray + _____ = _____
10. baby + _____ = _____

E

Each sentence has one misspelled word.
Write each word correctly on the blank.

1. They exchanged the other exportes for unrefined oil. _____
2. It would be foolish to copy an unprooven plan. _____
3. The bigest values are found in department stores. _____

Lesson 90 is a test lesson.
There is no worksheet.

Lesson 91

A

1. _____ 4. _____

2. _____ 5. _____

3. _____ 6. _____

B

Circle each short word that ends **cvc.**

1. reason	4. win	7. form	10. cover
2. stop	5. snap	8. fit	11. spin
3. grow	6. boy	9. stay	12. big

C

Add the morphographs together.

1. please + ing   = _____

2. worry + es   = _____

3. neat + ness   = _____

4. study + ed   = _____

5. sad + ness   = _____

6. re + late + ive = _____

7. story + es   = _____

8. fit + ing   = _____

9. pity + ful   = _____

10. wrap + er   = _____

Figure out the rules, and write them.

1. **c** in a short word when . . . morphograph begins with **v** . . . the word ends . . . Double the final . . . **cvc** and the next

_____

_____

2. a word when the word ends . . . next morphograph begins with anything except **i** . . . consonant-and-**y** and the . . . Change the **y** to **i** in

_____

_____

Lesson 92

1. _____
2. _____
3. _____
4. _____

5. _____
6. _____
7. _____

B

1. _____
2. _____
3. _____

4. _____
5. _____
6. _____

C

Make 11 real words from the morphographs in the box.

less	thought	ness	hope	ly	ful

1. _____
2. _____
3. _____
4. _____
5. _____
6. _____

7. _____
8. _____
9. _____
10. _____
11. _____

Complete each sentence correctly with these words:

write	**feat**	**their**	**hole**
whole	**vary**	**right**	**threw**

1. The detective thinks that she is not telling the _____ truth.

2. Jan swam across the raging river, which was a brave _____.

3. I used to print my name, but now I _____ it.

4. The restaurants on Miller Street are popular because they _____ their menus daily.

5. A strong man at the circus performed a different _____ of strength during every show.

6. The students checked _____ answers. Every student got every answer _____.

7. We _____ beanbags through a _____ in the wall.

Each sentence has one misspelled word.
Write each word correctly on the blank.

1. The queen stopped worying about her quest for _____
   golden things.

2. The children raced playfully into the swiming pool. _____

3. Suddenly we found out that we were near danjer. _____

A

1. _____
2. _____
3. _____

4. _____
5. _____
6. _____

B

1. _____
2. _____
3. _____
4. _____

C

power   doubt   price   guide   name   breath

D

Write contractions for the words below.

1. what is   = _____
2. would not = _____
3. can not   = _____
4. they have = _____

5. he will   = _____
6. are not   = _____
7. it is   = _____
8. they are   = _____

E

Add the morphographs together.

1. bench + es   = _____
2. try + es   = _____
3. nice + ly   = _____
4. early + er   = _____

5. copy + es   = _____
6. happy + ness = _____
7. worry + ed   = _____
8. stay + s   = _____

A

1. _____   4. _____

2. _____   5. _____

3. _____   6. _____

B

1. _____

2. _____

C

fashion   fair   solve   tribe   rich   globe

D

These words are in the puzzle.
Circle 7 or more of the words.

station	headed	stress
business	form	ruin
night	fires	meet
depart	equal	farms

m	h	s	s	f	f	f	f
m	e	e	t	t	o	i	a
d	e	p	a	r	t	r	r
r	q	t	t	d	e	e	m
b	u	s	i	n	e	s	s
h	a	i	o	s	s	d	s
s	l	i	n	i	g	h	t

E

Fill in the blanks to show the morphographs in each word.

1. _____ + _____ = request

2. _____ + _____ = powerful

3. _____ + _____ = conquest

4. _____ + _____ = varied

5. _____ + _____ = various

6. _____ + _____ = doubtless

7. _____ + _____ = lately

8. _____ + _____ + _____ = relation

F

Each sentence has one misspelled word.
Write each word correctly on the blank.

1. He was breething hard before the contest began. _____

2. The teacher asked the students to finnish their papers. _____

3. I wrote a story about a loveable athlete. _____

Lesson 95 is a test lesson.
There is no worksheet.

Lesson 96

A

Nineteen athletes exercised throughout the morning.

_____

_____

B

1. _____   4. _____

2. _____   5. _____

3. _____   6. _____

C

_____

_____

_____

_____

_____

_____

_____

_____

_____

Add the morphographs together.

1. danger + ous = _____

2. worth + y + ness = _____

3. quest + ion + able = _____

4. doubt + ful + ly = _____

5. probe + ing = _____

6. like + ly + ness = _____

7. re + solve = _____

8. note + ion = _____

9. carry + age = _____

10. fashion + able = _____

11. try + al = _____

12. con + tract + ion = _____

A

1. _____
2. _____
3. _____

4. _____
5. _____
6. _____

B

1. _____ + _____ = _____
2. _____ + _____ = _____
3. _____ + _____ = _____
4. _____ + _____ = _____
5. _____ + _____ = _____
6. _____ + _____ = _____

C

_ _ ete _ _ _t_ let _ _ _ _e_ c_ s_ _
_ _ _oug_ o_ _ ___ _or_ _ _ _.

_____

_____

D

Draw a line from each word to its clue.

would •	• in that place
there •	• My friends save _____ money.
here •	• We had a _____ good lunch.
hear •	• contraction of **they are**
very •	• How _____ you like a surprise?
plain •	• We expect better _____ tomorrow.
they're •	• Please speak louder. I can't _____ you.
their •	• in this place
weather •	• part of something
piece •	• ordinary

Lesson 98

A

1. _____
2. _____
3. _____
4. _____
5. _____
6. _____

B

1. _____ + _____ = _____
2. _____ + _____ = _____
3. _____ + _____ = _____
4. _____ + _____ = _____
5. _____ + _____ = _____
6. _____ + _____ = _____

C

D

_ _ _e_ _ _   _ _ _le_ _ _   _ _e_ c_ _ _ _

_ _ou_ _ _ _   _ _ _o_ _ _ .

_____

_____

E

Figure out the rules, and write them.

1. with anything except **i** . . . the next morphograph begins . . . **i** in a word when the . . . Change the **y** to . . . word ends consonant-and-**y** and

    _____

    _____

2. with **v** . . . morphograph begins . . . word when the next . . . final **e** from a . . . Drop the

    _____

    _____

F

Each sentence has one misspelled word.
Write each word correctly on the blank.

1. We could not believe her graceful baeuty.   _____

2. How piecefully the goats walked along the stony trail! _____

3. Be carefull not to misjudge what the class wrote.   _____

Lesson 99

A

scribe   store   fright   tough   short   loose

B

1. _____

_____

2. _____

_____

C

1. _ _ u b _

2. _ _ s h _ _ _

3. _ u _ _ _

4. _ o l _ _

5. _ o _ e _

6. _ _ _ _ _ i _ h _

D

Add the morphographs together.

1. un + fair + ly   = _____

2. drip + ing   = _____

3. hard + en + ed   = _____

4. room + y + ness   = _____

5. joy + ful + ly   = _____

6. un + de + feat + ed   = _____

7. tense + ion   = _____

8. in + tense + ive   = _____

9. glory + ous   = _____

10. pro + vise + ion   = _____

Lesson 100 is a test lesson.
There is no worksheet.

Lesson 101

A

script   tone   crease   shrink   tense   treat

B

People weren't interested in the photograph.

_____

_____

C

Complete each sentence correctly with these words:

their	**where**	**through**	**threw**
whether	**eight**	**loan**	**tale**

1. I had _____ good reasons for staying home.

2. They wanted to _____ me some money, but _____.
   pockets were empty.

3. We have to decide _____ or not we will go.

4. Mr. Samuels told us a _____ about a man who forgot
   _____ he lived one day.

5. We saw him _____ the window.

6. The girls _____ a few pebbles into the river.

7. Ivan and Roberta started _____ own business.

Add the morphographs together.

1. try + al = _____

2. con + tract + ion = _____

3. re + late + ive + ly = _____

4. city + es = _____

5. un + like + ly + ness = _____

6. ex + press + ion = _____

7. beauty + ful + ly = _____

8. noise + y + ness = _____

9. re + cent + ly = _____

10. in + cure + able = _____

11. un + ex + plain + ed = _____

12. re + late + ion = _____

Lesson 102

A

1. _____

2. _____

3. _____

4. _____

B

1. _____   4. _____

2. _____   5. _____

3. _____   6. _____

C

_____

_____

_____

_____

_____

_____

_____

_____

D

_ e o _ l _ _ _ r e ' _ _ t e r _ _ t _ _ _ _
_ _ _ p _ _ _ o _ _ _ p h .

_____

_____

E

Cross out the misspelled words in these sentences.
Then write the words correctly above the crossed-out words.

I could'nt here the teecher.

The whether has been beautyful this weck.

How many storys will the author right?

F

Each sentence has one misspelled word.
Write each word correctly on the blank.

1. We will replace the sourses of income we lost.   _____

2. They ignored our request for replasement parts.   _____

3. She spent hours wrapping those wonderful pakages.   _____

Lesson 103

A

1. _____ + _____ = _____
2. _____ + _____ = _____
3. _____ + _____ = _____
4. _____ + _____ = _____
5. _____ + _____ = _____
6. _____ + _____ = _____

B

1. _____
2. _____

C

D

_ _ o _ _ _   _ _ e _ _   _ _ e r _ _ _ _ _   _ _
_ _   _ _ _ _ _ _ _ p _ .

_____

_____

Write **s** or **es** in the second column.
Then add the morphographs together.

s or **es**   **s** or **es**

1. scratch + _____ = _____   5. fly   + _____ = _____

2. copy   + _____ = _____   6. hurry + _____ = _____

3. wash   + _____ = _____   7. dress + _____ = _____

4. boy   + _____ = _____   8. plan   + _____ = _____

Lesson 104

A

1. _____

_____

2. _____

_____

B

settle   agree   spirit   thirst   strict

C

1. _____   3. _____

2. _____   4. _____

D

Add the morphographs together.

1. un + in + form + ed   = _____

2. rate + ion   = _____

3. re + strict + ed   = _____

4. peace + ful + ly   = _____

5. fury + ous   = _____

6. re + late + ive + ly = _____

7. in + act + ive   = _____

8. study + ous   = _____

9. pro + port + ion   = _____

10. create + ive   = _____

E

Fill in the blanks to show the morphographs in each word.

1. _____ + _____ = snapping

2. _____ + _____ = rightful

3. _____ + _____ + _____ = depression

4. _____ + _____ + _____ = actively

5. _____ + _____ = various

6. _____ + _____ + _____ = proclaimed

F

Each sentence has one misspelled word.
Write each word correctly on the blank.

1. Tom was finally defeeted in the last contest.   _____

2. The quiz had some questions I couln't answer.   _____

3. We questioned the soundness of their statments.   _____

Lesson 105 is a test lesson.
There is no worksheet.

Lesson 106

Anybody would rather be healthy instead of rich.

_____

_____

B

1. _____   3. _____

2. _____   4. _____

C

1. _____   3. _____

2. _____   4. _____

D

Write the correct spelling for each word.

Then write one of these letters after each number:

Write **O** if the word is spelled by just putting the morphographs together.

Write **A** if the final-**e** rule explains why the spelling is changed.

Write **B** if the doubling rule explains why the spelling is changed.

Write **C** if the **y**-to-**i** rule explains why the spelling is changed.

1. _____ hurry + ed   = _____

2. _____ carry + ing   = _____

3. _____ trap + er   = _____

4. _____ happy + ness = _____

5. _____ ease + y   = _____

6. _____ proud + ly   = _____

7. _____ late + ly   = _____

8. _____ tense + ion   = _____

9. _____ clap + ing   = _____

Lesson 107

A

_____o__ _oul_ _a__er __
_eal___ ____ea_ __ __c_.

_____

_____

B

Write the correct spelling for each word.
Then write one of these letters after each number:

Write **O** if the word is spelled by just putting the morphographs together.
Write **A** if the final-**e** rule explains why the spelling is changed.
Write **B** if the doubling rule explains why the spelling is changed.
Write **C** if the **y**-to-**i** rule explains why the spelling is changed.

1. _____ low + er   = _____
2. _____ snap + ed   = _____
3. _____ store + age   = _____
4. _____ edge + y   = _____
5. _____ slip + ing   = _____
6. _____ move + ment   = _____
7. _____ fit + ness   = _____
8. _____ flaw + ed   = _____
9. _____ note + ion   = _____
10. _____ play + ing   = _____
11. _____ run + y   = _____
12. _____ like + able   = _____

Circle the misspelled word in each group.
Then write it correctly on the line.

1. fashion
   poison
   strate
   rather

   _____

2. glory
   pleaze
   place
   settle

   _____

3. brother
   wrong
   carry
   hopeing

   _____

4. prove
   cawse
   hurried
   agree

   _____

5. crease
   change
   request
   ninteen

   _____

6. choice
   sorce
   strength
   studying

   _____

7. sturdyness
   recover
   serve
   priceless

   _____

8. swimmer
   serving
   pitiful
   lowwer

   _____

Fill in the blanks to show the morphographs in each word.

1. _____ + _____ + _____ = repressive
2. _____ + _____ + _____ = depression
3. _____ + _____ + _____ = expressed
4. _____ + _____ = feature
5. _____ + _____ + _____ = defeated
6. _____ + _____ = passion
7. _____ + _____ + _____ = profoundly
8. _____ + _____ + _____ = invaluable

Lesson 108

A

Write **s** or **es** in the second column.
Then add the morphographs together.

s or **es**

1. press + _____ = _____
2. shop + _____ = _____
3. buzz + _____ = _____
4. box + _____ = _____
5. stretch + _____ = _____
6. rich + _____ = _____
7. wash + _____ = _____
8. script + _____ = _____

B

_ _ _ _ _ o _ _ _ _ _ _ _ _ _ _ _ _ _ e _ _ _

_ _ a _ _ _ _ _ _ _ _ _ a _ _ _ _ _ _ _ _.

_____

_____

C

1. _____   4. _____

2. _____   5. _____

3. _____

D

Write the correct word from each sentence.

1. The **weather/whether** has been great. _____

2. They found **their/there** things. _____

3. We **through/threw** rocks in the lake. _____

4. Pat ate **to/too** much. _____

5. Please bring those books **hear/here**. _____

E

Fill in the blanks to show the morphographs in each word.

1. _____ + _____ = poisonous

2. _____ + _____ = famous

3. _____ + _____ = relate

4. _____ + _____ + _____ = relative

5. _____ + _____ + _____ = reaction

6. _____ + _____ + _____ = expression

A

duty   danger   round   speak   fury   seize

B

1. _____

_____

2. _____

_____

C

1. _____   4. _____

2. _____   5. _____

3. _____

D

Write **s** or **es** in the second column.
Then add the morphographs together.

1. tax   + _____ = _____

2. brush + _____ = _____

3. claim + _____ = _____

4. waltz + _____ = _____

5. pass + _____ = _____

6. light + _____ = _____

7. reach + _____ = _____

8. rich + _____ = _____

Add the morphographs together.

1. deny + al = _____

2. glory + ous = _____

3. press + ure = _____

4. mis + con + cept + ion = _____

5. un + ex + cept + ed = _____

6. flaw + ed = _____

7. thirst + y = _____

8. ex + press + ion = _____

9. in + ject + ion = _____

10. seize + ure = _____

Each sentence has one misspelled word.
Write each word correctly on the blank.

1. Who knows whether the whether will change soon. _____

2. The riseing water caused damage and defaced the land. _____

3. She explaned her plan for bringing about peace and reform. _____

Lesson 110 is a test lesson.
There is no worksheet.

Lesson 111

1. _____
2. _____
3. _____

4. _____
5. _____

B

C

Make 9 real words from the morphographs in the box.

est	mad	happy	ly	wide	ness	fine

1. _____
2. _____
3. _____
4. _____
5. _____

6. _____
7. _____
8. _____
9. _____

Fill in the blanks to show the morphographs in each word.

1. _____ + _____ + _____ = protective

2. _____ + _____ + _____ = injected

3. _____ + _____ + _____ = progressed

4. _____ + _____ + _____ = reception

5. _____ + _____ = texture

6. _____ + _____ + _____ = featuring

7. _____ + _____ = passion

8. _____ + _____ = studying

9. _____ + _____ = studious

10. _____ + _____ = signal

Each sentence has one misspelled word.
Write each word correctly on the blank.

1. They were surprised by the gloryous cities they _____
discovered.

2. They expresed delight over the unexpected outcome. _____

3. Everybody who was on duty felt frightened and edgey. _____

Lesson 112

The union of physical science and logic was a major development.

_____

_____

s or **es**

1. worry + _____ = _____
2. play + _____ = _____
3. try + _____ = _____
4. joy + _____ = _____
5. copy + _____ = _____
6. boy + _____ = _____
7. story + _____ = _____
8. study + _____ = _____
9. stay + _____ = _____
10. duty + _____ = _____

1. _____   4. _____

2. _____   5. _____

3. _____

Add the morphographs together.
Remember to use your spelling rules.

1. danger + ous = _____

2. seize + ure = _____

3. fury + ous = _____

4. script + ure = _____

5. quest + ion + able = _____

6. poison + ous = _____

7. fur + y = _____

8. please + ure = _____

9. friend + ly + ness = _____

10. re + fuse + al = _____

E

Cross out the misspelled words in these sentences.
Then write the words correctly above the crossed-out words.

Could you speak a little lowder, please?

Where are the fameous people?

Their was no reeson for the rejection.

Lesson 113

_ __ __ i o __ __ __ y s ____
___ e _ c _ ___ _ o g __ ___
_ __ j o _ __ __ e _ o _____ .

_____

_____

1. _____   5. _____

2. _____   6. _____

3. _____   7. _____

4. _____   8. _____

s or **es**

1. boy   + _____ = _____

2. story + _____ = _____

3. try   + _____ = _____

4. worry + _____ = _____

5. baby + _____ = _____

6. fly   + _____ = _____

7. berry + _____ = _____

8. carry + _____ = _____

1. _____

2. _____

3. _____

4. _____

5. _____

E

These words are in the puzzle.
Circle 7 or more of the words.

poison found photo

pound concept flat

lone   pity   whose

store   fact   proven

p	p	w	h	o	s	e	f
p	o	i	s	o	n	s	p
c	o	n	c	e	p	t	r
f	o	u	n	d	h	o	o
a	l	o	n	e	o	r	v
c	p	a	r	d	t	e	e
t	p	i	t	y	o	e	n

Lesson 114

A

___ _____ __ _____
_____ __ ____ __
_ ____ _____.

_____

_____

B

1. _____

_____

2. _____

_____

C

1. _____   4. _____

2. _____   5. _____

3. _____   6. _____

Write **s** or **es** in the second column.
Then add the morphographs together.

1. worry + _____ = _____
2. pinch + _____ = _____
3. truck + _____ = _____
4. story + _____ = _____
5. copy   + _____ = _____
6. poison + _____ = _____
7. study + _____ = _____
8. cry   + _____ = _____

E

Complete each sentence correctly with these words:

whole	write	hole	features
varies	right	weather	morning

1. Caron's experiment failed, but she had the _____ idea.
2. Tony is going to _____ a short story.
3. Our boat won't float because it has a large _____ in it.
4. I can't eat a _____ cake.
5. Murphy's Cafe _____ fried chicken every Friday.
6. Robin exercises every _____.
7. The _____ in Trinidad rarely _____.
8. Tahiti _____ great _____.

> This is the last worksheet in Level D.
> There are no student worksheets for Lessons 115—120.

Word List

word	lesson	word	lesson	word	lesson	word	lesson	word	lesson
a	21	big	46	buzzes	107	choppy	17	consign	29
above	52	biggest	12	by	62	cities	86	consignment	54
act	41	blackness	87	can	104	city	53	constrict	31
action	88	bliss	47	can't	56	civil	33	constricted	38
active	84	blissful	12	care	3	civilly	33	contacted	77
actively	90	bloomed	46	cared	24	claim	32	contain	114
agree	104	blow	39	careful	26	claims	32	contest	43
all	119	blowing	53	carefully	21	clapping	42	context	42
am	63	boat	22	careless	3	class	54	contract	42
an	14	boats	26	carelessly	18	classes	28	contracted	54
answer	7	boldness	6	carriage	96	close	13	contraction	96
answers	67	book	56	carried	29	clothes	12	copied	26
anybody	106	box	28	carrier	56	cloud	3	copier	24
are	59	boxes	32	carries	82	clouded	8	copies	82
aren't	58	boxing	32	carry	18	cloudiest	53	copy	24
arms	24	boy	17	carrying	38	cloudiness	46	copying	25
asked	116	boyish	56	catch	22	cloudless	1	could	42
at	94	boyishness	8	catches	28	clouds	66	couldn't	57
athlete	71	boys	68	caught	7	cloudy	17	count	64
athletes	96	brain	51	cause	47	coat	22	counting	71
author	6	break	6	cent	50	coats	27	countless	86
authoring	11	breakable	39	chain	51	coin	42	cover	73
babies	82	breath	93	chalk	12	cold	42	crashes	28
baby	42	breathe	57	change	33	coldly	11	crease	101
babyish	59	breathing	94	changes	69	come	56	create	104
backs	24	bridge	101	changing	33	coming	66	creative	104
bar	37	brief	77	charge	9	concept	106	cried	61
bare	37	briefest	81	charging	9	confine	33	crier	28
bared	24	briefly	79	charm	52	confined	57	cries	82
baring	24	brother	37	cheap	2	confinement	49	cry	28
barred	54	brotherly	67	cheapest	2	confining	41	crying	34
base	45	brown	67	chief	77	confirmed	42	curable	7
basement	51	brownish	16	chiefly	81	conform	29	cure	46
be	51	brush	48	child	3	conformed	72	danger	73
beautiful	77	brushes	27	childish	18	conforming	31	dangerous	94
beautifully	83	build	1	childishly	21	confront	29	dark	58
beauty	73	building	1	childishness	74	confronted	71	darken	12
before	71	bush	49	childless	3	confuse	42	darkness	6
believe	44	bushes	29	children	32	confused	51	date	27
bench	12	busiest	64	choice	1	confusing	41	day	102
benches	32	business	62	choicest	54	conjecture	108	deal	59
berries	113	busy	11	choke	51	conquest	94	dealer	26
berry	17	busyness	62	choking	6	consent	48	deception	112
best	22	buzz	37	chop	52	conserve	39	deceptive	106

Word List

word	lesson	word	lesson	word	lesson	word	lesson	word	lesson
defacing	63	dining	24	eight	46	feature	106	fool	16
defeat	61	disease	28	else	71	features	114	foolish	16
defeated	71	dish	28	enough	57	featuring	111	foolishly	38
define	11	dishes	28	equal	2	feel	41	for	59
defined	11	does	56	equally	22	feet	6	force	37
defining	35	doesn't	58	error	46	fell	79	forceful	54
dejected	108	door	14	especially	82	fight	6	forcefully	37
delight	11	dosage	42	everyone	71	fighter	29	form	14
delighted	27	dose	42	except	107	final	14	formal	14
delightful	3	doubt	93	exception	113	finally	27	formally	26
denial	31	doubtful	116	exchange	62	fine	6	former	72
denied	26	doubtfully	96	exchanging	77	finely	16	formless	29
dented	41	doubtless	94	exciting	82	finest	6	forms	28
deny	26	drag	12	exclaim	66	finish	81	found	42
denying	63	dragging	12	exercise	106	finished	71	fox	28
depart	11	drain	51	exercised	96	fire	22	foxes	33
departed	12	drainage	57	explain	85	fired	22	freshen	12
department	49	dress	18	explained	68	fires	94	friend	29
deport	19	dresses	29	export	62	firm	42	friendliest	63
deported	43	dressy	18	exported	67	first	79	friendliness	29
depressed	39	dried	28	exports	89	fish	69	friendly	42
depressing	33	drink	33	express	62	fit	12	friends	24
depression	92	drip	16	expressed	107	fitness	12	fright	99
describe	113	dripped	16	expression	93	fitting	91	from	81
deserve	33	dripping	51	expressive	88	flame	41	front	37
deserved	21	drive	103	fact	113	flat	9	frost	18
design	26	driving	103	fail	34	flatly	14	frosty	18
designed	36	drop	14	fair	94	flatten	42	fudge	24
designer	21	dropped	98	fame	108	flattest	31	funny	21
desk	48	dropper	14	famous	94	flaw	108	fur	18
desks	41	dropping	28	fanciest	29	flawed	107	furious	27
detain	114	dry	28	fanciful	27	flier	56	furry	18
detect	107	drying	30	fancy	18	flies	83	fury	109
detecting	106	dull	63	farm	9	float	22	fuse	41
detection	112	duties	112	farmer	9	floated	54	gain	51
detective	107	duty	109	farming	16	floating	42	girl	33
detract	51	earlier	53	farms	29	flop	12	girlishness	33
development	112	earliest	49	fashion	94	flopping	12	glass	28
did	24	early	46	fashionable	96	flow	39	glasses	28
didn't	58	ease	28	fatally	42	flower	54	global	19
different	13	easily	39	fate	42	flowers	46	globe	19
dine	56	easy	27	fault	22	fluid	42	glories	86
dined	24	edge	107	faultless	3	fly	22	glorious	97
diner	24	edgy	107	feat	4	flying	41	glory	4

Word List

word	lesson	word	lesson	word	lesson	word	lesson	word	lesson
goat	22	healthy	106	in	101	largest	8	loud	67
goats	27	hear	8	inactive	90	late	22	louder	112
going	68	heard	22	income	66	lately	22	loudest	68
gold	27	heaviest	69	incurable	37	latest	59	loudly	66
golden	19	heavy	57	inflaming	41	law	88	lovable	9
gone	56	he'll	57	inform	28	leader	44	love	9
good	59	help	8	informal	28	leak	41	low	39
govern	79	helped	8	informed	43	leakage	41	lower	98
government	83	helpful	2	informer	33	leakages	71	luck	31
grab	16	helpfully	14	inhuman	31	leave	32	luckily	53
grabbed	16	helpless	120	injected	111	length	18	lucky	31
grace	22	helplessly	62	injection	108	lengthen	51	lunch	29
graceful	22	helplessness	8	inland	28	lengthening	47	lunches	29
gracefully	29	her	22	inside	33	lengthy	23	mad	11
great	114	here	3	instated	42	let's	59	madden	46
greatest	62	he's	54	instead	106	light	2	madder	41
greatness	53	him	43	instilled	41	lighten	12	maddest	13
grief	77	hired	57	insure	42	lighter	64	madly	11
grip	77	his	94	intake	28	lightest	2	madness	12
gripped	118	hit	22	intended	58	lighting	2	main	32
gripping	77	hole	17	intensive	99	lightly	11	mainly	44
ground	69	hope	7	interested	101	lights	27	maintain	114
grow	39	hoped	44	into	117	likable	7	major	112
grudge	9	hopeful	24	invaluable	37	like	6	make	41
guide	93	hopefully	26	investment	52	likeliest	29	many	102
gum	17	hopeless	7	investments	53	likeliness	33	mark	27
gummy	17	hopelessly	11	is	32	likely	41	mash	22
had	28	hopelessness	14	isn't	57	likeness	6	match	56
happier	24	hoping	13	it	32	likes	102	matches	27
happiest	32	hot	22	it's	54	listen	1	me	38
happily	33	hotly	33	I've	56	listened	8	meet	94
happiness	26	hotter	86	joy	22	listening	1	mess	29
happy	2	hottest	66	joyful	59	load	57	messes	29
hard	57	house	43	joyfully	64	loan	36	might	8
hardened	99	huge	64	joyous	24	lock	4	mighty	21
harm	27	human	24	joys	82	locked	14	misconception	109
harmless	118	humans	24	judge	22	logic	112	misjudge	22
harmlessly	27	hurried	26	jumpy	17	lone	32	misplaced	39
hasn't	54	hurries	103	kindness	43	loneliest	63	misprinted	58
hate	22	hurry	23	know	24	loneliness	41	misquote	4
have	102	hurrying	39	lake	81	lonely	37	misquoted	21
haven't	59	I	28	landed	66	long	83	misshaped	11
he	38	if	118	large	8	longer	9	misspell	4
headed	94	I'll	61	largely	64	loose	99	misspelled	82

Word List

misspelling....... 19	notion 96	pinch............... 14	preserve........... 43	purest 13
mistake 4	nudge 71	pinches 29	preserved......... 19	quest............... 68
mistaken 27	nudging 71	pitied............... 33	preserving......... 9	question............. 7
misuse 27	of 42	pitiful.............. 24	press 28	questionable.... 51
morning 96	off 79	pity 21	presses 28	questions......... 26
mother 54	often 69	pitying............. 46	pressure......... 106	quick............... 68
mothering 54	on 34	place 12	preview 9	quickest 86
motoring 31	one................. 71	placement........ 49	previewed 27	quickly 73
motors 28	other 81	plain............... 47	prewash............. 9	quiet................. 6
movable.......... 64	our 46	plan 17	prewrap 59	quieter 9
move............... 32	pack............... 13	plane 48	price............... 93	quietest............. 7
movement........ 49	package 13	planned 33	print 58	quietly 11
mover 66	packages 102	planner........... 31	probe 96	quietness.......... 6
moving 42	packaging 61	planners 36	probing 96	quite............... 69
nail 34	paint 8	planning........... 17	proclaim........... 82	quiz............... 68
nails 38	painted 53	plans 103	proclaimed..... 104	quotable 11
name............... 93	painter 37	plants............. 29	profile............. 82	quote 2
namely 96	paints 34	play 17	profound 96	quoting 6
nastier............. 86	part 12	played 44	profoundly 83	race................. 43
nastiest 86	parts 24	player 26	progress 106	races 43
nastily 86	pass 109	playful 24	progressed 106	racing 31
neat................. 32	passage 13	playfully 47	progression.... 107	rage 59
neatly 33	passes 27	playing 79	progressive 109	raging 59
neatness 91	passion 107	plays 82	project 108	rail................... 36
nerve............... 32	passive 84	please 7	projecting....... 112	rain................. 33
nervous.......... 103	patch 34	pleasing 24	projection....... 114	rainy............... 17
nice.................. 9	patches........... 34	pleasure......... 112	prolong 82	rather 106
nicely 29	pause 47	point 58	prolonged 83	ration 104
nicer................. 9	pay................. 23	pointless 39	proportion...... 104	reach............... 32
niece 77	payment........... 49	points............. 28	protect 107	reaches 32
night 94	peace............. 71	poison............. 47	protection 107	react 64
nightly 77	peaceful 71	poisoning 76	protective....... 111	reacting............ 41
nights 29	peacefully 77	poisonous........ 97	proud 67	reaction........... 88
nineteen........... 96	people.............. 4	poisons 114	proudly 106	read 41
noise 11	person 12	port 6	prove 13	real................. 22
noisiness.......... 68	personal........... 19	portable 7	proven 24	really 22
noisy 19	personally 46	pound 113	proverb 88	reason............. 79
norm 16	photo 113	power 93	proving............ 21	reasonable....... 83
normal 16	photograph.... 101	powerful.......... 94	provision 99	reasons........... 89
normally........... 33	physical 112	predated 27	prowl............. 67	rebuild.............. 1
not 24	picture 7	preplanned 33	pup 18	rebuilding.......... 6
notable............ 14	pictures........... 34	preschool........ 43	puppy 18	recently 66
note 13	piece.............. 74	present 9	pure 13	reception 107
noted 98	pills 24	presented 18	purely............. 21	receptive......... 106

word	lesson	word	lesson	word	lesson	word	lesson	word	lesson
recover	79	replacement	71	rise	66	search	1	skid	97
refine	38	replacing	91	risen	8	searched	1	skidded	97
refined	14	report	67	rising	66	searching	1	skipping	8
refinement	56	reported	64	robber	56	second	82	slam	41
reformed	16	reporter	27	room	81	seize	109	slammed	41
reformer	72	repression	88	roominess	99	seizure	109	sleep	2
refresh	74	repressive	106	rooms	26	self	17	sleeping	1
refreshed	19	request	71	rose	17	selfish	16	sleepless	3
refreshes	74	requesting	76	rosy	17	selfishly	17	sleeplessness	7
refreshing	120	research	1	roughest	64	selfishness	18	sleepy	17
refreshment	51	researcher	21	round	69	sent	48	slice	52
refreshments	71	researches	74	ruin	42	serve	9	slightly	77
refusal	112	reservation	52	ruined	46	served	24	slip	107
regained	68	reserve	19	run	11	server	24	slipping	92
regress	107	reserved	37	runner	11	serving	11	slow	42
regressing	106	reserving	63	running	12	settle	104	smile	62
reinform	72	resign	33	runny	107	several	12	snail	34
reinformed	72	resigned	54	sack	22	shape	11	snap	37
reinstate	31	resolve	96	sad	9	shaping	120	snapped	107
reject	108	resort	36	sadden	14	she	21	snapping	104
rejecting	107	resource	3	saddening	64	she'll	58	snug	9
rejection	109	resourceful	14	sadder	63	she's	57	snugness	42
relate	49	resources	74	saddest	11	shine	8	solve	94
related	23	rest	22	sadly	11	shining	8	some	21
relation	93	restful	26	sadness	16	shiny	17	sore	6
relative	84	restfully	26	safe	21	ship	58	soreness	6
relatively	101	restless	26	safely	21	shipment	58	sort	1
remain	37	restlessly	26	safest	54	shop	22	sorted	8
remaining	38	restlessness	23	sail	22	shopper	17	sound	57
remark	7	restore	96	sailboat	11	shopping	24	soundly	63
remarkable	7	restricted	77	sailboats	81	shops	24	soundness	66
removal	42	retain	114	sailing	59	short	38	sounds	68
remove	71	retract	43	sale	51	should	33	source	3
removed	56	review	1	saw	14	shouldn't	54	sources	53
removing	56	rewrap	90	school	6	show	39	south	67
rent	16	rich	94	schools	27	shrink	101	speak	14
rental	14	riches	108	science	112	sick	31	speaker	16
rented	24	right	2	scratch	29	side	33	speech	33
renter	24	rightful	98	scratched	64	sign	2	speeches	27
renting	24	rightfully	61	scratches	49	signal	37	speed	58
repack	1	ring	1	scribe	99	signs	24	speediest	58
repainted	8	ripe	6	script	101	skate	18	speedy	106
replace	43	ripeness	7	scripts	108	skating	21	spell	3
replaced	12	ripest	6	scripture	112	sketch	11	spelling	3

Word List

Word List

word	lesson	word	lesson	word	lesson	word	lesson	word	lesson
unwashable	8	voice	8	we	22	winners	48	worthiness	96
unwrap	13	volt	18	weather	39	wire	18	worthless	13
usable	8	voltage	38	week	102	wiry	18	worthy	31
usage	19	wake	52	we'll	61	wishes	29	would	38
use	8	waltz	109	were	62	won	99	wouldn't	56
useful	26	waltzes	109	we're	56	wonder	23	wrap	13
useless	8	wander	1	weren't	58	wondered	51	wrapped	98
uselessly	26	wandered	29	we've	56	wonderful	48	wrapper	13
using	104	wandering	1	what	51	wonderfully	23	wrapping	56
valuable	19	warm	18	what's	59	wondering	43	wreck	13
value	18	warmest	18	where	120	wood	79	wreckage	13
varied	31	was	56	whether	43	woods	22	write	1
varies	114	wash	8	which	86	work	68	writing	8
various	94	washable	7	who	56	world	9	wrong	7
vary	21	washes	28	whole	16	worldly	21	wrote	38
verb	88	wasn't	54	whose	32	worlds	74	yellow	17
verbal	14	watch	41	wide	11	worried	27	you	17
verbally	66	watched	93	widely	11	worrier	63	you'll	54
very	26	watches	46	widest	12	worries	82	your	38
vest	52	watching	84	will	102	worry	27	you're	61
view	1	water	12	win	21	worrying	32	you've	58
viewing	1	watering	12	winner	21	worth	13		

Study Lists

build
building
care
cheap
cheapest
child
childless
cloud
cloudless
equal
glory
happy
light
lightest
lighting
listen
listening
lock
misquote
people
quote
rebuild
repack
research
resource
review
right
search
sign
sleep
sleepless
sort
source
spell
spelling
straight
straightest
stretch
stretching
study
unequal
uneven

unhappy
view
wander
wandering
write

6-10

answer
author
boldness
break
careless
caught
charge
charging
choice
choking
clouded
curable
darkness
farmer
fight
finest
grudge
helped
helplessness
hopeless
largest
likable
likeness
listened
longer
lovable
might
mistake
nicer
picture
please
port
portable
present
preserving
preview

prewash
question
quiet
quieter
quietest
quietness
quoting
rebuilding
remarkable
repainted
ripeness
ripest
school
searching
serve
shining
sleeping
sleeplessness
soreness
sorted
staging
story
stretchable
stretched
style
styled
thought
thoughtlessness
timeless
together
unbreakable
unending
unwashable
usable
useless
voice
washable
world
writing
wrong

11-15

authoring

bench
biggest
blissful
busy
chalk
coldly
darken
define
defined
delight
delightful
depart
departed
different
dragging
final
fitness
flopping
formal
freshen
helpful
helpfully
here
hopelessly
hopelessness
hoping
lighten
lightly
madly
madness
misshaped
noise
notable
note
package
passage
person
pinch
prove
pure
purest
quietly
quotable
refined

rental
replaced
resourceful
runner
running
saddest
sadly
sailboat
serving
several
sketch
speak
starred
stopped
straighter
swimming
thoughtful
thoughtlessly
through
twice
unequally
unlikely
unproven
verbal
watering
widely
widest
worthless
wreck
wreckage

16-20

brownish
carelessly
carry
childish
choppy
cloudy
dressy
dripped
fancy
farming
finely

Study Lists

foolish
frosty
furry
global
golden
grabbed
gummy
hole
jumpy
length
misspell
misspelling
noisy
normal
personal
planning
presented
preserved
puppy
rainy
reformed
refreshed
reserve
rosy
sadness
selfish
selfishly
selfishness
shiny
shopper
skate
sleepy
speaker
spinning
starring
stony
storable
straighten
strength
strengthen
sturdy
sunny
swimmer
thoughtfulness

tribal
unneeded
usage
valuable
value
warmest
whole
wiry
wrapper

21-25

bared
baring
biggest
cared
carefully
childishly
coat
copied
copying
deserved
designer
dined
diner
dining
equally
faultless
fired
float
fudge
funny
goat
graceful
hopeful
lately
lengthy
mighty
misjudge
nice
pitiful
playful
pleasing
proven

proving
purely
really
related
rented
renter
renting
researcher
restlessness
safely
sail
served
server
shopping
skating
spotless
stately
stepping
stylish
teacher
throat
trace
unplanned
vary
winner
wonderfully
worldly

26-30

arms
boats
box
brushes
bushes
careful
carried
catches
classes
coats
conform
confront
consign
crashes

crier
dealer
delighted
denied
design
disease
dishes
dresses
dried
dropping
drying
easy
fanciest
fanciful
farms
fighter
finally
formally
formless
forms
fox
friendliness
friends
glasses
goats
gracefully
happiness
harmlessly
hopefully
hurried
inform
informal
inland
intake
lights
likeliest
lunches
matches
messes
mistaken
motors
nicely
nights
pinches

plants
player
points
predated
presses
previewed
questions
reporter
restful
restfully
restless
restlessly
rooms
sadden
schools
scratch
shops
speeches
stars
stayed
stretches
studied
studying
sturdier
sturdiness
tails
tax
trips
trying
unpreserved
useful
uselessly
very
washes
wishes
worried

31-35

benches
boxes
boxing
changing
children

Study Lists

civilly
claim
claims
confine
conforming
constrict
crying
defining
degrade
denial
depressing
deserve
fail
foxes
girlishness
happiest
happily
hotly
informer
inhuman
inside
leave
likeliness
lone
lucky
maddest
main
motoring
move
nail
neat
neatly
normally
patches
pitied
planned
planner
preplanned
reaches
reinstate
resign
sick
signs
snail

sprayed
stitches
taxes
trail
trapper
tried
turn
unclaimed
undrinkable
unlikeliness
varied
whose
worrying
worthy

36-40

blow
breakable
carrying
conserve
depressed
easily
flow
foolishly
forcefully
grow
incurable
invaluable
know
loan
lonely
low
misplaced
nails
pointless
rail
refine
remain
remaining
reserved
show
sturdiest
throw

tricky
unclear
uninformed
voltage
weather

41-45

clapping
confining
confirmed
confusing
contest
context
contract
dosage
fatally
flatten
flattest
fluid
flying
hoped
inflaming
instated
instilled
leader
leakage
loneliness
moving
played
races
reacting
removal
retract
ruin
slammed
snugness
spray
stylishly
text
tract
undefeated
unlucky
unreadable

whether

46-50

bloomed
boyishness
cause
cloudiness
confinement
consent
darkness
department
earliest
early
flowers
informed
lengthening
madden
movement
our
pause
payment
personally
placement
plain
playfully
poison
relate
ruined
scratches
spotted
statement
strange
strangely
stranger
strangest
toughest
trailer
watches
winners
wonderful
yellow

51-55

barred
basement
choicest
cloudiest
consignment
contracted
detract
drain
earlier
forceful
gain
hasn't
he's
investment
investments
it's
luckily
mothering
questionable
rain
refreshment
resigned
safest
sale
shouldn't
signal
sources
sprain
stain
stained
strangeness
taken
unconfirmed
unmistakable
wasn't
you'll

56-60

aren't
babyish
boyish

Study Lists

breathe
can't
carrier
confined
couldn't
didn't
doesn't
drainage
flier
hard
haven't
heavy
he'll
intended
isn't
I've
joyful
latest
let's
light
load
make
misprinted
painter
prewrap
raging
refinement
removed
removing
rewrap
she'll
she's
shipment
speediest
strained
sure
they'll
they're
touched
trial
uncivilly
unsnapped
unvaried
we're

weren't
we've
what's
wouldn't
wrapping
you've

61-65

busiest
business
busyness
cried
defacing
denying
exchange
export
express
friendliest
greatest
helplessly
I'll
it's
let's
loneliest
packaging
remark
reserving
rightfully
saddening
sadder
scratched
she's
soundly
strengthening
their
unequally
unrefined
unrelated
unsturdy
we'll
worrier
you're

66-70

brown
count
exclaim
explained
exported
ground
heaviest
hottest
income
loudly
mainly
mover
noisiness
proud
prowl
quest
quick
quiz
recently
regained
rising
round
soundness
sounds
south
town
undeserving
verbally

71-75

athlete
beauty
before
conformed
confronted
counting
danger
defeated
else
everyone
finished

former
it's
let's
nudging
one
peace
racing
reformer
reinform
reinformed
replacement
request
sudden
that's
wondered

76-80

beautiful
brief
chief
contacted
exchanging
first
govern
grief
gripping
house
largely
niece
nightly
peaceful
peacefully
reason
requesting
restricted
roughest
slightly
suddenly
thief
type
unquotable
unrecoverable

81-85

active
babies
beautifully
boys
briefest
briefly
carries
chiefly
copies
cries
especially
exciting
explain
flies
government
joys
passive
plays
proclaim
profile
profoundly
prolong
prolonged
relative
second
sprays
stays
stories
studies
surprise
threw
toys
trapped
tries
uncovered
untyped
worries

86-90

action
actively

Study Lists

blackness
cities
expressive
glories
hotter
inactive
nastier
nastiest
nastily
proverb
react
reaction
reasonable
reasons
repression
station
sturdily
they'd
thoughts
watching

91-95

breath
conquest
dangerous
depression
doubt
doubtless
expression
fair
famous
fashion
fitting
globe
guide
joyous
name
neatness
power
powerful
price
relation
replace

rich
slipping
solve
stepped
they've
thoughtfully
thoughtless
tribe
various
what's

96-100

athletes
carriage
changes
contraction
derailed
doubtfully
dripping
dropped
exercised
fashionable
fright
glorious
hardened
intensive
joyfully
loose
morning
namely
nineteen
notion
poisoning
poisonous
probing
profound
provision
quickest
resolve
restore
rightful
roominess
scribe

short
skidded
store
tension
throughout
tough
tripped
unfairly
worthiness

101-105

agree
crease
creative
driving
furious
hurries
interested
nervous
photograph
plans
proclaimed
proportion
ration
relatively
script
settle
shrink
snapping
spirit
strict
studious
tense
thirst
tone
treat

106-110

anybody
buzzes
concept
conjecture

deceptive
deforming
dejected
detect
detecting
detective
duty
edgy
except
expressed
feature
flawed
fury
healthy
injection
instead
lower
misconception
passes
playing
poisoned
pressure
progress
progressed
progression
progressive
project
protect
protection
proudly
rather
reception
receptive
regress
regressing
reject
rejecting
rejection
repressive
rich
riches
runny
scripts
seize

seizure
snapped
speedy
texture
thirsty
treatment
unexcepted

111-115

berries
contain
deception
detain
detection
development
duties
exception
exercise
featuring
helpless
injected
logic
maintain
major
passion
physical
pleasure
poisons
preserve
projecting
projection
protective
retain
refreshing
science
scripture
shaping
sport
trucks
union
where

Spelling Rules

Lesson	Rule	Explanation
6	**Final-E Rule**	When do you drop the final **e** from a word? When the next morphograph begins with a vowel letter.
11	**Doubling Rule**	When do you double the final **c** in a short word? When the word ends **cvc** and the next morphograph begins with **v.**
17	**Y as a Vowel**	When is **y** a vowel letter? At the end of a morphograph.
24	**Y-to-I Rule**	When do you change the **y** to **i** in a word? When the word ends with a consonant-and-**y** and the next morphograph begins with anything except **i.**
27	**E-S Endings**	If a word ends in **s, sh,** or **ch,** you add **e-s** to make the plural word.
32	**E-S Endings**	If a word ends in **x,** you add **e-s** to make the plural word.
82	**E-S Endings**	If a word ends with a consonant-and-**y,** you add **e-s** to make the plural word.
88	**W as a Vowel**	When is **w** a vowel letter? At the end of a morphograph.
107	**E-S Endings**	If a word ends in **z,** you add **e-s** to make the plural word.

Meanings of Affixes and Nonword Bases

Morphograph	Lesson	Meanings	Examples
-able	7	can be	stretchable, washable, readable
-age	13	result of an action	package, usage, marriage
-al	14	related to, like	formal, trial, rental
cept	106	to take; contain	receptive, intercept, acceptable
con-	29	with, together	conform, contest, condense
de-	11	down, away from; reverse of; remove from	deport, deform, depart
-ed	8	(action) in the past	formed, stepped, cried
-en	12	to make	loosen, darken, straighten
-er	9	more; one who	greater, lighter; teacher, dancer
-es	27	more than one; a verb marker for *he, she,* or *it*	lilies, boxes; watches, catches
-est	2	the most	greatest, lightest, happiest
ex-	62	out, away	export, exclude, extend
-ful	12	full of; tending to	careful, beautiful; forgetful
gress	106	to step	regression, progress, transgression
in-	28	in, into; not; really	include; incurable; invaluable
-ing	1	when you do something, ongoing action	spending, moving, stopping
-ion	88	state, quality, act, or process	action, taxation, repression
-ish	16	like, related to, inclined to be	babyish, stylish, boyish, greenish
-ive	84	quality of; one who	expressive, informative; relative, detective
ject	107	to throw	rejecting, dejected, projection
-less	3	without	painless, useless, restless

Meanings of Affixes and Nonword Bases

Morphograph	Lesson	Meanings	Examples
-ly	11	how something is done	quietly, equally, basically
-ment	49	result of doing something	placement, requirement, apartment
mis-	4	wrongly	misspell, misjudge, misprint
-ness	6	that which is, quality of	quietness, freshness, thickness
-ous	94	having the quality of	famous, furious, joyous
pre-	9	before	preview, preclude, prepay
pro-	82	in favor of; before; forward	proclaim; provision; progress
re-	1	again, back	rerun, return, replace
-s	24	more than one; a verb marker for *he, she,* or *it*	friends, bananas, farmers; acts, writes, talks
tain	114	to hold	retaining, container, detained
tect	106	to cover	detecting, protection
un-	2	not, the opposite of	unhappy, unusual, untie
-ure	106	act, process	departure, pressure, failure
-y	17	having the quality of; belonging to	shiny, dreamy, mighty

Contractions

Component Words	Contractions	Component Words	Contractions
are not	aren't	she will	she'll
can not	can't	should not	shouldn't
could not	couldn't	they are	they're
did not	didn't	they had	they'd
does not	doesn't	they have	they've
has not	hasn't	they will	they'll
have not	haven't	was not	wasn't
he is	he's	we are	we're
he will	he'll	we will	we'll
I have	I've	were not	weren't
I will	I'll	what is	what's
is not	isn't	would not	wouldn't
it is	it's	you are	you're
let us	let's	you have	you've
she is	she's	you will	you'll

ate	refers to:	eat in the past
	example:	I *ate* a sandwich.
eight	refers to:	the number 8
	example:	The dog had *eight* puppies.

close	refers to:	shut something
	example:	Please *close* the door.
clothes	refers to:	things you wear
	example:	They bought lots of *clothes*.

feat	refers to:	something that is hard to do
	example:	Climbing the mountain was a great *feat*.
feet	refers to:	body parts
	example:	Her *feet* were sore from running.

for	refers to:	in place of
	example:	She went to the store *for* me.
four	refers to:	the number 4
	example:	Cats have *four* legs.

hear	refers to:	listen
	example:	I can't *hear* you.
here	refers to:	this place
	example:	Come over *here*.

hole	refers to:	empty space
	example:	I have a *hole* in my sock.
whole	refers to:	entire, complete
	example:	He ate the *whole* pie.

loan	refers to:	allow to borrow something
	example:	She will *loan* me lunch money.
lone	refers to:	by itself
	example:	There was a *lone* tree.

meat	refers to:	food from animals
	example:	Some people don't eat *meat*.
meet	refers to:	come together
	example:	We agreed to *meet* next week.

peace	refers to:	calm; no war
	example:	I like *peace* and quiet.
piece	refers to:	a part
	example:	I ate a *piece* of fruit.

plain	refers to:	simple; ordinary
	example:	She wore a *plain* black dress.
plane	refers to:	flat surface or air transportation
	example:	The *plane* landed safely.

right	refers to:	correct or opposite of left
	example:	All my answers were *right*. She wears a ring on her *right* hand.
write	refers to:	put words on paper
	example:	You must *write* neatly.

sail	refers to:	travel on water in a ship or a boat
	example:	We learned how to *sail* at camp.
sale	refers to:	available to buy or an offer at a cheaper price
	example:	Our house is for *sale*. He bought the shoes on *sale*.

tail	refers to:	the back end
	example:	The dog chased his *tail*.
tale	refers to:	a story
	example:	He told an interesting *tale*.

continued on next page

Homonyms

their   refers to: belonging to them
           example: It is *their* house.

there   refers to: that place
           example: Go over *there.*

they're refers to: they are
           example: I think *they're* ready.

---

threw   refers to: throw in the past
           example: She *threw* the ball.

through refers to: in one side and out the other
           example: We went *through* the tunnel.

---

vary   refers to: change
           example: His moods *vary* from day to day.

very   refers to: really, quite, especially
           example: That story is *very* imaginative.

---

wear   refers to: have clothes on your body
           example: What shall I *wear* today?

where   refers to: what place
           example: *Where* do you want to go?

---

weather refers to: what it feels like out of doors
           example: Always wear a hat in cold *weather.*

whether refers to: if
           example: I don't care *whether* I go or not.

---

wood   refers to: what trees are made of
           example: We need *wood* for the fire.

would   refers to: what might happen
           example: I *would* like to go to Paris.

---

your   refers to: belonging to you
           example: *Your* coat is blue.

you're refers to: you are
           example: *You're* ready.

Test Charts

	Lesson 5	Lesson 10	Lesson 15	Lesson 20	Lesson 25	Lesson 30	30-Lesson Total
Super Speller	25	25	25	25	25	25	
	24	24	24	24	24	24	
	23	23	23	23	23	23	
Very Good Speller	22	22	22	22	22	22	138 = Super Speller
	21	21	21	21	21	21	
	20	20	20	20	20	20	
	19	19	19	19	19	19	
	18	18	18	18	18	18	
	17	17	17	17	17	17	
	16	16	16	16	16	16	
	15	15	15	15	15	15	
	14	14	14	14	14	14	
	13	13	13	13	13	13	
	12	12	12	12	12	12	
	11	11	11	11	11	11	
	10	10	10	10	10	10	
	9	9	9	9	9	9	
	8	8	8	8	8	8	
	7	7	7	7	7	7	
	6	6	6	6	6	6	
	5	5	5	5	5	5	
	4	4	4	4	4	4	
	3	3	3	3	3	3	
	2	2	2	2	2	2	
	1	1	1	1	1	1	

Test Charts

	Lesson 35	Lesson 40	Lesson 45	Lesson 50	Lesson 55	Lesson 60	30-Lesson Total
Super Speller	25	25	25	25	25	25	
	24	24	24	24	24	24	
	23	23	23	23	23	23	**138 = Super Speller**
Very Good Speller	22	22	22	22	22	22	
	21	21	21	21	21	21	
	20	20	20	20	20	20	
	19	19	19	19	19	19	
	18	18	18	18	18	18	
	17	17	17	17	17	17	
	16	16	16	16	16	16	
	15	15	15	15	15	15	
	14	14	14	14	14	14	
	13	13	13	13	13	13	
	12	12	12	12	12	12	
	11	11	11	11	11	11	
	10	10	10	10	10	10	
	9	9	9	9	9	9	
	8	8	8	8	8	8	
	7	7	7	7	7	7	
	6	6	6	6	6	6	
	5	5	5	5	5	5	
	4	4	4	4	4	4	
	3	3	3	3	3	3	
	2	2	2	2	2	2	
	1	1	1	1	1	1	

Test Charts

	Lesson 65	Lesson 70	Lesson 75	Lesson 80	Lesson 85	Lesson 90	30-Lesson Total
Super Speller	25	25	25	25	25	25	
	24	24	24	24	24	24	
	23	23	23	23	23	23	
Very Good Speller	22	22	22	22	22	22	138 = Super Speller
	21	21	21	21	21	21	
	20	20	20	20	20	20	
	19	19	19	19	19	19	
	18	18	18	18	18	18	
	17	17	17	17	17	17	
	16	16	16	16	16	16	
	15	15	15	15	15	15	
	14	14	14	14	14	14	
	13	13	13	13	13	13	
	12	12	12	12	12	12	
	11	11	11	11	11	11	
	10	10	10	10	10	10	
	9	9	9	9	9	9	
	8	8	8	8	8	8	
	7	7	7	7	7	7	
	6	6	6	6	6	6	
	5	5	5	5	5	5	
	4	4	4	4	4	4	
	3	3	3	3	3	3	
	2	2	2	2	2	2	
	1	1	1	1	1	1	

Test Charts

	Lesson 95	Lesson 100	Lesson 105	Lesson 110	Lesson 115	Lesson 120	30-Lesson Total
Super Speller	25	25	25	25	25	25	
	24	24	24	24	24	24	
	23	23	23	23	23	23	
Very Good Speller	22	22	22	22	22	22	**138 = Super Speller**
	21	21	21	21	21	21	
	20	20	20	20	20	20	
	19	19	19	19	19	19	
	18	18	18	18	18	18	
	17	17	17	17	17	17	
	16	16	16	16	16	16	
	15	15	15	15	15	15	
	14	14	14	14	14	14	
	13	13	13	13	13	13	
	12	12	12	12	12	12	
	11	11	11	11	11	11	
	10	10	10	10	10	10	
	9	9	9	9	9	9	
	8	8	8	8	8	8	
	7	7	7	7	7	7	
	6	6	6	6	6	6	
	5	5	5	5	5	5	
	4	4	4	4	4	4	
	3	3	3	3	3	3	
	2	2	2	2	2	2	
	1	1	1	1	1	1	